A Beginner's Guide to Ogham Divination

A Beginner's Guide to Ogham Divination

Ceri Norman

MOON BOOKS

Winchester, UK
Washington, USA

JOHN HUNT PUBLISHING

First published by Moon Books, 2022
Moon Books is an imprint of John Hunt Publishing Ltd., No. 3 East Street, Alresford
Hampshire SO24 9EE, UK
office@jhpbooks.net
www.johnhuntpublishing.com
www.moon-books.net

For distributor details and how to order please visit the 'Ordering' section on our website.

Design: Matthew Greenfield

UK: Printed and bound by CPI Group (UK) Ltd, Croydon, CR0 4YY
Printed in North America by CPI GPS partners

We operate a distinctive and ethical publishing philosophy in
all areas of our business, from our global network of authors to
production and worldwide distribution.

Contents

Disclaimer

The information given as part of this book is strictly for educational and entertainment purposes. In absolutely no way is it meant as a substitute for proper medical diagnosis and treatment by registered healthcare professionals. It is very strongly recommended that you consult a licensed healthcare practitioner for any physical or psychological ailments you may have.

Introduction

My aim in writing this book is to inspire you to find and create your own practical and meaningful way of working with the magic and mystery of the ancient Celtic Ogham and its trees, for both divination and as a part of your daily life and spiritual practice – if you have one. Once upon a time the Ogham was considerably more than the tree alphabet we know it as today. Many people are drawn to the Ogham precisely because they feel a deep affinity for trees, so the focus of this book is on its associated trees. I have also endeavoured to include their original meanings and other useful information to assist you.

This book is not a history text on the ancient Ogham and does not claim to be. Instead, I have allowed the history of the Ogham and the old sources that give us the meanings behind each of its symbols, as well as later folklore and legend, to inspire this work and the meaning given within it for each of the trees. Trees are amazing, and I hope to share my deep love of and reverence for trees with you in a way that can help you to build up your own meaningful relationship with trees and with Nature, which is all around us if we know where to look.

I wish you every success with the Ogham and with the future.

Part I

Chapter 1

The Letters, Legends and Lore of the Ogham

The Ogham is an ancient magical and mysterious alphabet, the letters of which are closely associated with various trees, as well as a vast storehouse of ancient wisdom. It is much more than just a series of letters though, for the letters, or *Fews,* are essentially keys that unlock the mysteries, metaphysics, magic and mythology of the Forest and the wider Universe, and provide invaluable insight into what is going on inside our own heads and hearts. Each letter has a myriad of associations, such as a tree, a bird, a craft, a colour, a saint, a king, a body of water, a type of person, and a whole lot of lore and legends. The Ogham has a lot to teach us. All we need to do is listen and learn.

The Letters of the Ogham Alphabet

The Beith Aicme	The Huathe Aicme	The Muinn Aicme	The Ailm Aicme	The Forfeda
Beith Birch	Huathe Hawthorn	Muinn Bramble	Ailm Pine	Ehhadh Elecampane
Luis Rowan	Duir Oak	Gort Ivy	Onn Gorse	Oir Spindle
Fearn Alder	Tinne Holly	Ngeadal Broom	Ur Heather	Uillean Honeysuckle
Saille Willow	Coll Hazel	Straif Blackthorn	Edhadh Aspen	Iphin Gooseberry
Nuinn Ash	Quert Apple	Ruis Elder	Idho Yew	Eamhancholl Wych Elm

Technically the word *Ogham* only refers to the physical form of the letters, the letters or alphabet itself is known as *Beith-Luis-*

3

Nin, the first part is named for the first two letters, Beith (Birch) and Luis (Rowan), while the third part, *Nin*, refers to a 'forked branch', so may in fact mean something akin to 'letter'. This is exactly the same idea as with the name for the Roman alphabet in which you are reading this book, which takes its name from its first two letters: *alpha* and *beta*.

The letters themselves were historically called *Feda* 'Wood' or 'Tree', or *Nin* meaning 'Forked Branch' but these days are known as *Fews* or occasionally as *Fees*. The form of Ogham is unique; the twenty original letters are put into four *Aicmi* (*Aicmi* is the plural, *Aicme* the singular) which are groups or families of five. Each group is named after the first letter of its group. There was a later addition of five extra characters to account for linguistic changes, which are very different in appearance to the others. These extras are known as the *Forfeda* or 'Additions'.

The Ogham script is a series of notches or lines called *Flesc* or 'Twig' which are carved or written along a central line called the *Druim*. Dots are frequently used between words and spaces between letters. The letters are traditionally written from the roots up, from bottom to top, and from left to right.

The wands, twigs, and markers used in Ogham divination, upon which the Few is depicted, are known as Ogham Staves. The word Stave, just like the Fews of the Ogham, is loaded with multiple meanings. Stave may refer to a stanza or portion of poetry, the lines upon which music is written, a supportive walking stick, a magical staff, or a magical sigil. An Ogham Stave is metaphorically and metaphysically all of these things in one.

Mythical Origins

There are two legends about the creation of the Ogham which differ considerably. One is Pagan, the other is Christian.

According to *The Book of Invasions* and *The Scholar's Primer*, Ogham was invented by the Scythian King, Fenius Farsa. The story goes that Fenius, along with Goídel mac Ethéoir, Íar mac Nema and dozens of other scholars journeyed from Scythia to the Tower of Babel in order to study the confusion of tongues – the Biblical explanation for why there are so many different languages spoken around the globe. Once they arrived, they found that the confused languages had already spread out all over the world and so Fenius sent his Academics out far and wide to study the new languages, while he co-ordinated all their efforts from the Tower of Babel. After ten years Fenius created what became known as 'the selected language' which apparently took the best of each of the other languages to form a new language, which he named Goidelic after his trusted ally Goídel mac Ethéoir. In order to have a way of writing and further communicating this new language, Fenius also created the Ogham, also known as *Beith-Luis-Nin*. The names Fenius gave to the twenty-five letters that he created were either the names of his twenty-five best performing scholars or the names of trees.

According to *The Ogham Tract*, the inventor of the Ogham was Ogma – the Irish God of Eloquence and Poetry. The very first message ever written in Ogham were seven 'B's on Birch bark that were sent to the God Lugh as a warning that his wife would be carried away to the Otherworld seven times unless she was protected by the Birch tree. This is explained as being the reason that the first letter of the Ogham is named for the Birch tree and ultimately why all the letters are named for trees.

Ogma's name, and the name of the Ogham alphabet itself, derive from the Indo-European root word *'ag-'* meaning 'to cut' and the Ogham was indeed cut into wood and stone. Ogma was one of the Tuatha Dé Danann, a mythical, godlike race who once inhabited Ireland. Ogma was known by three epithets which provide us with insight into his character: *Grianaineac* ('Sun-Faced'), *Cermait* ('Honey-Tongued') and *Trenfher* ('Strongman').[1] *The Book of Ballymote* tells us that: *'Ogma, much skilled in dialects and poetry, as proof of his intellect, invented Ogham for signing secret speech known only to the learned to the exclusion of rustics and herdsmen'.* This makes it clear that the use of Ogham was originally limited to the Druid and elite classes.

Ogma was a God of the Druids; his Ogham was an essential part of the curriculum at the Druidic Training Colleges, and in the training of Gaelic poets, where students had to learn one hundred and fifty types of Ogham, fifty in each of their three years of study. Our ancestors saw writing as magical, to them it appeared from the Otherworld as a gift from the Divine. Prior to the invention of writing the only method of passing on information was by word of mouth, but writing has the power to carry information across distances and even time. Even after the advent of writing the Druids appear to have had a bit of an aversion to it, because they traditionally placed such great value on learning everything by heart and that is why so much of their wisdom has since been lost.

Historical Origins

Ogham is indeed thought to have been created by one man, although we do not know his name, somewhere around between 600 BCE and 300 CE and there is a lot of arguing amongst experts as to the approximate date. The history of Ogham is a bit of a mystery; there is no evidence to suggest that it existed before the Roman era and the structure of the alphabet appears to have been borrowed from Latin and/or Greek. Perhaps a learned person of Ireland decided to create their own writing form, based on the Roman/Greek one. The Celts certainly had no problems borrowing from other cultures, but any borrowings were usually fully integrated into their own Celtic culture.

There are three main theories as to why the Ogham was created:

1. It was created and designed as an esoteric and cryptic alphabet by Druids or Pagan Irish scholars for religious,

political or even military purposes.[2] The idea is that this alphabet, being very different from the Latin one, would allow the Irish to communicate without the Romans understanding what was being said. We have to remember that at this time the Roman Empire had conquered much of England and was considered a very genuine threat to Ireland.

2. The Ogham was created by the first Christian communities that were established in Ireland. This theory puts forward the fact that the sounds of the Irish language were hard to put into Latin letters and so the Christians created their own writing system that would work with the Irish language.[3]

3. The Ogham was originally invented by Gaulish Druids as a secret system of hand signals. This is meant to explain why the letters are grouped in fives and display between one and five lines in the form of a tally, after all we have five digits on each hand. According to this version, the Ogham was first created in around 600 BCE and not used as a writing system until much later, and even then, was first used on perishable materials like birch bark, before it was carved into stone.

Sources

The first evidence that we have of the Ogham in use are the stone inscriptions which are known as the Orthodox inscriptions, that date from between the fourth and sixth centuries CE. These feature only twenty letters. Some of these inscriptions have been successfully translated, others have not. Those which have been translated tend to be territorial markers or memorial stones rather than anything esoteric. Considering we do not know what the others say, and some do appear very cryptic, we cannot say for certain whether they are just mere markers or are in fact something more magical…

The later inscriptions, dating from the sixth to tenth century CE are known as the Scholastic Inscriptions and can include up to twenty-five letters. The Ogham itself is predominantly found in Ireland, where there have been recorded over three hundred Ogham Inscriptions in stone, mostly in Southern Munster, but its influence spread to other Celtic lands, there are around forty Ogham inscriptions in Pembrokeshire in Wales, thirty-four in Scotland, seven in England and five on the Isle of Man.[4]

Much of our knowledge about the meanings and associations of the Ogham alphabet is derived from later sources, from the Scholastic Ogham of the sixth to ninth centuries CE. Most of these are manuscripts, and some claim to have been based on earlier manuscripts than those which have survived, hence the term Scholastic.

Auraicept na n-Éces or *'The Scholar's Primer'* is a highly prized source of information on the Ogham. *The Scholar's Primer* is originally thought to date from around the mid-seventh century CE, although the earliest copy we have of it is found in *Leabhar Bhaile an Mhóta* or *'The Book of Ballymote'* and is dated to around 1390 CE. This is the earliest record of the idea that the twenty-five letters were named after trees and also records actual uses of the trees, as types of firewood, cattle fodder, what can be made from them, what insects or animals might hide in them, or just simple descriptions of the trees.

In Lebor Ogaim or *'The Book of Ogams'*, better known today as *The Ogham Tract* is a treatise on the Ogham alphabet that is also found in *The Book of Ballymote*, but is a separate entity to *The Scholar's Primer*. Again, while our earliest copy of this work dates to the fourteenth century CE, the original work appears to be older. *The Ogham Tract* records over one hundred secret ways of writing and working with the Ogham, some of which are more akin to tallying, while others are various lists of words based on the letters. According to *The Ogham Tract* the Tree Ogham is just one of almost a hundred Oghams. Others include the Colour Ogham, Bird Ogham, Agricultural Ogham, Art Ogham, People Ogham, etc. These may have been mnemonic devices to assist in learning vast amounts of information.

The Ogham Tract includes ways of signalling or passing on secret messages with the Ogham, such as the Nose Ogham, where you sign the letter by using the fingers of your hand against your nose or the Ogham of Interwoven Thread which shows ways on encoding the Ogham Fews into cloth. It is also from *The Ogham Tract* that we learn of a specific method of divination involving the letters of the Ogham, which we will look at later.

Bríatharogam or *'Word Oghams'* are High Mediaeval word kennings that explain the meanings of the names of the letters of the Ogham alphabet. Very little is known about their origin and confusingly there are actually two different versions of one of them. The first two are found in *The Scholar's Primer* and so must date back at least to the fourteenth century CE, but the third is not found until much later documents from the seventeenth century CE.

There are three of these *Word Oghams*:

- Bríatharogam Morainn mac Moín ('The Word Ogham of Morann Mac Main')
- Bríatharogam Maic ind Óc ('The Word Ogham of Maic ind Óc or Oenghus')
- Bríatharogam Con Culainn ('The Word Ogham of Cuchulainn')

The three *Word Oghams* contain similarities and differences.

9

Each has a very different angle and reflects the aspects and personality of the person to whom they are accredited, although we do not know if they actually composed them. Morann Mac Main was a famous judge and poet, his Ogham is the most straightforward of the three. Cuchulainn was a famous warrior hence the abundance of references to battle and death. Oenghus' are vaguer and poetic, this is not surprising as he was said to have enjoyed riddles. I include *The Word Oghams* for each of the Fews in their own section so you can read and examine them as you ponder the traditional meaning of each tree and what each of the trees means to you personally.

De Dúilib Feda Na Forfed or *'Of the Feda Elements of the Forfeda'* is a very short work that talks of the five extra letters, the diphthongs, that were added later to the original twenty.

Chapter 2

The Ogham and Trees

The Celtic Tree Alphabet

Most of us today know of the Ogham as 'The Celtic Tree Alphabet' although trees are only one part of this very complex system. Indeed, Ogham Fews are often now named after and associated with trees, though this was not always the case. It seems that at some point in the past a Tree Alphabet and the Ogham were fused together. In modern Gaelic the letters of the alphabet are very occasionally still, somewhat archaically, referred to by their tree names.

We do not know when the blending of The Tree Alphabet and the Ogham happened, but we do know that it seems to be before the fourteenth century CE because both *The Scholar's Primer* and *The Ogham Tract* assign names of trees to each of the letters. *The Ogham Tract* tells us *'It is from the trees of the forest that names were given to the Ogham letter metaphorically'.*[5] That said, *The Ogham Tract* actually acknowledges that this was not the case in the past, when in fact only about half of the Fews or letters were named for trees, bushes and the like. The others were named for quite random things such as the colour red, an iron ingot, sulphur and even a type of sound.

The original letters that were always named for trees, plants and their ilk are *Beith* ('Birch'), *Luis* ('Herb'), *Fearn* ('Alder'), *Saille* ('Willow'), *Duir* ('Oak'), *Coll* ('Hazel'), *Quert* ('Bush'), *Onn* ('Ash', which then became 'Gorse') and *Idho* ('Yew' or 'Evergreen'). Of the five Forfeda only two are named for trees and such, *Iphin* ('Spiny') and *Eamhancholl* ('Twin of Hazel').

Even once all of the twenty-five letters had been assigned trees, much confusion remained, even in the same document. Here, then, are some examples of this confusion from within

11

The Ogham Tract:

> It is recorded in one place that the Yew is Idho, then later it is recorded as Edhadh.
> Uillean is described as both Ivy and Honeysuckle.
> Hawthorn is recorded as both Huathe and Ur.
> Gort is described as both Ivy and as a Cornfield.

This is why you will often find different trees assigned to certain letters by different modern authors. The truth is that no one is wrong, we are all just working from different parts of the same old source.

The letters themselves became known as *Nin* ('Forked Branch') or *Feda* ('Twig'), the notches used to create them are called *Flesc* ('Twig') and represent the branches of a tree and the central line or Druim represents the trunk of a tree.

The Celtic Tree Calendar

In recent times the Ogham has become intricately linked to what is called *The Celtic Tree Calendar*. This calendar has nothing to do with the ancient Celts and was an imaginative construct by the twentieth-century CE writer, researcher and Revivalist, Robert Graves, who having read the work of a seventeenth-century CE Bard, Roderick O'Flaherty, convinced himself that the names of the Ogham letters contained a calendar, a liturgy of the Pagan God and Goddess and the codification of the ancient lore and wisdom of the Celts and Druids. Ogham's revival in the twentieth century CE is due in part to Robert Graves' work, especially *The White Goddess*, which is an interesting book, but needs to be taken with a large pinch of salt. In it Graves is looking at equating his knowledge of Classical Mythology with Celtic Mythology, and showing parallels between them. In its own way it is a very important book within the Celtic Revival and modern Paganism, and it has given us some fascinating insights into the Ogham and how it can be imaginatively interpreted.

The concept of *The Celtic Tree Calendar* is that the thirteen Moons of the year are represented by thirteen trees, and so followed the lunar cycle rather than having set dates. Sometimes you may hear these thirteen trees called the lunar trees. Then for practical reasons the dates of the thirteen months became fixed.

The Modern Pagan Festivals were also assigned a tree, as were the mysterious end days of Midwinter, between the Winter Solstice on 21st December when the Sun is seen to standstill in its rising and setting positions and Old Yule on the 24th of December when the days visibly start to lengthen again. These trees may sometimes be referred to as the Solar trees.

Regardless of its origins and history, or lack thereof, the pattern of *The Celtic Tree Calendar* is quite well designed and thought through. Each one of the trees is indeed doing something particularly interesting around the time it has been assigned, and so seems to emphasise its presence and power during that Moon or month. For example, the Hawthorn flowers during its time of May 13th to June 9th, the Bramble and the Apple have their berries and apples at their ripest during their time of September 2nd to 29th, and the catkins of the Willow are at their best during its assigned time of April 15th to May 12th.

Some like to use *The Celtic Tree Calendar* in their work with the Ogham because it gives them another way to connect magically and energetically to the trees and offers us a potential time frame when we are divining with the Ogham, while others shun it because it is not genuinely historical. It is completely your choice as to whether or not you use it, adapt it to suit your needs or completely ignore it, but just in case I have provided the relevant information for you under each Few and handy graphic here:

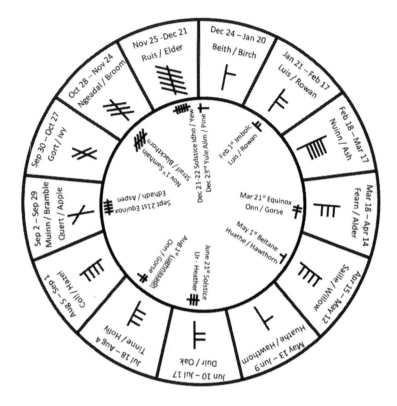

The Celtic Perception of Trees

That the Ogham became associated with trees is no surprise, for the Celts have long revered and respected trees. In Irish they even have a special word for a 'Sacred Tree' – *Bile*. The first-century CE Roman writer, Pliny, recorded that the Druids of Old practiced their rites in woodland groves, especially those of Oak. It is also worth noting that according to The Living Tree Foundation in Sneem, County Kerry, out of the approximate 16,000 towns in Ireland, around 13,000 are named after trees. That is over eighty percent!

As well as the original sources of the Ogham we can learn a lot about how the Celts and their descendants viewed specific types of trees, and what energies and abilities they were credited with, from several other sources:

Cad Goddeu ('The Battle of the Trees') is a fourteenth-century CE Welsh poem in which the Magician Gwydion brings the trees of the forest alive in order to fight as his private army. Each tree is given a little description as to its conduct which alludes to its perceived personality and energy. Where relevant I have added the corresponding line of this poem to the information for each tree. Many Celtic Revivalists and modern Druids believe that the role of each tree in the poem relates to the Ogham and therefore, that ancient Druidic wisdom regarding trees is stored within the poem. Others dispute this, but either way there is something quite powerful about this fascinating poem that echoes our primal fear of, and enchantment with, trees.

The Song of Amergin is a supposedly very ancient poem, dating back to before the time of the Roman Conquest of Britain. The earliest recorded version of the Song is found in the twelfth-century CE Irish manuscript, *Lebar na Núachongbála* ('The Book of Leinster'). Amergin was a Bard and Judge for the Milesians of Irish Legend who sought to take Ireland from the Tuatha Dé Danann. They achieved their victory because Amergin called upon the spirit of the land of Ireland itself with a powerful magical incantation that has since become known as The Song of Amergin. Within the song, Amergin states many things, but towards the end he makes five statements that appear to tally with the five vowels and Fews of the Ailm Aicme, and in their relevant order, which seems to be more than a mere coincidence: *'I am the womb of every holt,* (reference to Ailm or Pine who holds the newly born Midwinter Sun).

> *I am the blaze on every hill,* (refers to Onn or Gorse when it is in full flower)
> *I am the queen of every hive,* (a reference to Ur or Heather which is much loved by bees)
> *I am the shield for every head,* (refers to Edhadh or Aspen which

15

was famous for its use for shields)

I am the tomb of every hope.[6] (a reference to Idho or Yew that symbolises death and the tomb)

Bretha Comaithchesa ('Judgements of Neighbourhood') is an eighth-century CE code within the Brehon Laws of Ireland which governed the everyday life of Mediaeval Ireland. The judgements outlay the offences that a farmer might commit against a neighbour, including damage to the neighbour's trees. Not only is the damage itself placed into four distinct classes, the trees themselves are placed into four specific classes based on their perceived worth: the Chieftain Trees, the Commoner Trees, The Lower Divisions and Shrubs. Damage to the Chieftain Trees, such as Oak or Hazel was considered a far more serious transgression that damaging a Lower Division Tree. Under each of the trees, you will find their class listed according to these judgements.

Celtic Mythology is rich in mentions of trees. Certain deities were associated closely with certain types of trees, such as the Welsh King and God Bran the Blessed who was associated with the Alder, Lugh who carried a spear made with Holly and the Irish Goddess and Saint Brighid who was associated with the Oak.

Folklore and Superstitions tell us a lot about how people view trees. There are some considered lucky and others that are considered unlucky. Certain trees are associated with healing, while others are said to be linked to death.

Dendrolatry ('The Worship of Trees') from around the World can teach us a great deal about how ancient cultures engaged with, worshipped and revered trees. As trees grow so high into the air and so deep into the earth, they were seen to connect the Heavens, the Underworld and our World and allow communication between these different realms. Sacred groves and trees can be referenced in most mythologies and in most countries all over the planet. At such places people communed with their Gods and the spirits. In Mesopotamian mythology the Cedar Forest is the realm of the Gods.[7] In Japan many Shinto sites are sacred groves or are based around them, the Druid's communed with their Deities in groves of Oak, the Vikings made sacrifices to their Gods at the Uppsala Grove in Sweden. Sometimes the Gods talked back, such as with the Oracle of Dodona, where Zeus, the King of the Gods, spoke to his devoted followers through the rustling of the leaves of an ancient oracular Oak tree.[8] This tree could not only speak of the words and wisdom of Zeus courtesy of its great canopy that reached up in to the sky, it was also reputed to be able to speak of the mysteries of the Underworld for its equally great network of roots was said to reach all the way down to Tartarus.[9] In slightly later times it is also interesting to note that divination was performed at Dodona, as indeed it was throughout the ancient world, by the casting of wooden lots.

Our Modern Perception of Trees

Today there seem to be two general perceptions of trees. For some they are simply resources, they are things to make furniture, medicines, paper, and other material goods from, and this attitude to trees is why there are far fewer of them today than there were in times past. For others, trees are incredible, awe-inspiring and majestic living beings which have so much to offer and teach us. In many ways it is this second attitude that connects us most deeply with how our ancestors viewed trees, although they were not averse to hewing them down. What is truly fantastic is that modern science and ongoing scientific discoveries are revealing some amazing and mind-bending things about trees that fully support the idea that trees are intelligent and amazing beings.

Trees are still loved, revered, and in some cases still worshipped, even today. Companies and schools may take their names or create their logos with trees, or their leaves and fruits because they want to embody something of that tree or invoke its powers. Some parents still name their children after trees, Rowan, Willow, Heather, Holly and Hazel are all quite popular names at the moment and many of our surnames, as well as place names, derive from various trees.

Trees can give us a sense of belonging and a sense of place. As someone who has spent a lot of time in various parts of the UK and Scandinavia growing up, I was always very aware of the differences in what grew in the different areas that I either lived in or visited. The local trees seemed to help give its place its uniqueness and its energy. When I think back on those places and those times, the trees are what jump out at me. For example, for me, Suffolk, in England, was a place of the Pine and the golden Gorse, South Wales was the land of Wild Garlic and the Oak tree, the island of Møn in Denmark was a place of the Beech, and Dalarna in Sweden was a place of the Birch. Many countries still have national or regional trees: Wales, England, Ireland, Poland, Serbia and the United States all have the Oak, Scotland has the Scot's Pine, North Korea and South Korea each have their own different type of Pine, Japan has the Cherry, Sweden, Finland and Russia have the Birch and Ukraine has the Willow.

Physically and mentally trees and humans have much in common and we are finding more of these commonalities all the time thanks to both science and spirituality. Trees and humans communicate through networks which have a staggeringly similar concept and appearance. We both breathe and have an interdependent relationship on what we each breathe in and out: we need the oxygen they exhale when we inhale and they breathe in the carbon dioxide that we exhale. Trees are the lungs of the planet and our own lungs with all their little airways strongly resemble the branches or roots of the tree. We also stand upright like the tree and our physical forms consist of trunks, a crown and limbs. We both have roots, in our case our roots define where we have come from, in terms of both location and the families that created us – it's no coincidence that we call the visual representation of our lineage 'our family tree'. Both trees and humans need certain things to survive and as science has recently discovered, we are both capable of communication, caring for and supporting our young and each other, and we both have strong senses of smell and taste.

Trees are still providing for and supporting us, not only in the form of oxygen, but also as building materials, paper, furniture, medicines and shelter. Recently humankind has realised just how important trees are to combating the effects of climate change for trees can help to prevent flooding, landslides, store carbon and to cool our ever-warming air. Trees are vitally important to well-being of the planet and all the life is supports, which includes humans.

Trees and forests continue to inspire creative souls everywhere. Music, dance, artworks, poetry and prose are all still continually being inspired by them and created in their honour. Tree lover, Naturalist and Poet, Henry David Thoreau, once declared the tree to be *'living poetry'*[10].

People still use trees in our rituals and ceremonies. We plant trees and forests to commemorate events, such as the birth of a child or the passing of a loved one, or to commemorate the millennium. Trees may also serve as memorials for those lost to terrorist attacks or disasters, such as the Survivor Tree at the Oklahoma City National Memorial, which survived the Oklahoma bombing in 1995. Woodland burials are also becoming increasingly popular.

People still love and want to be near trees. Humans have a strong desire to live in areas with trees. Commercial areas with trees also attract far more customers than those without.

Woodlands are places we journey to for recreation and for healing. Woodlands and wooded parks are among the most popular destinations for tourism all over the world.

We are also rediscovering the amazing medicinal and healing properties of trees, not just in terms of the medicines they can provide us with, but in the sense of healing that their mere presence inspires. I say rediscovering because this is not a new concept at all. In the sixth century BCE, Cyrus the Great, founder of the first Persian Empire, ordered the planting of a garden in the midst of Pasargadae – his capital city, to promote the well-being of the residents. In the sixteenth century CE, Paracelsus wrote: 'The art of healing comes from nature, not from the physician.' Then in 1982 CE, Tomohide Akiyama, who worked for the Japanese Ministry of Agriculture, Forestry and Fisheries created *Shinrin-yoku* ('Forest Bathing' or 'Forest Therapy') to encourage more people to visit forests, which has since become popular all over the world. In Japan and South Korea, it has become a prescribed therapy for those with depression, anxiety or Post-Traumatic Stress Disorder.

Trees are therapists. Walking or just sitting in woodlands or other green areas has been proved to improve our sense of well-being. Being with trees reduces our levels of stress and anxiety, leaving us feeling relaxed and at peace. Crucially, trees, being much larger and older than ourselves, help us to shift our perspective. We are able to perceive and connect with something far bigger and greater than ourselves. Trees help us to achieve a state of mindfulness and awareness, which enables to be more aware of ourselves, our surroundings and the greater planet and Cosmos. By becoming more aware of this we come to care more about it and so trees have helped inspire many people to try and take better care of the planet.

For many people it is their love of trees or a specific tree that inspires them to become interested in saving the planet or advocating for the environment. When these beloved trees are threatened, people seem to spring into action to try and protect them. It does not always work, but once inspired the interest in such activism seems to continue. Trees and other forest beings have also been known to convert foresters and even loggers to their cause. Our modern environmental ethics and the modern American ideas of wilderness preservation are borne out of the work of the once forester and later conservationist, Aldo Leopold. The mycologist, Paul Stamets (who the *Star Trek: Discovery* character is named after) started out as a logger, felling trees for a living, but had his interest in nature piqued by the fungi he encountered. Stamets' interest and subsequent research has completely revolutionised how we view fungi, trees and forests as a whole.

Trees have gifted us wisdom in many ways. In the Germanic and Celtic languages there are several words related to wisdom that derive from the root word of *vid/wit* and *wydd* respectively, both meaning 'wood'. These include *witiga* ('wisdom'), *witan* ('wise men' and the name of the assembly who counselled the King in Anglo-Saxon England). We can still find its influence in modern English in the words Dr*uid*, *Wit*ch or *Wiz*ard. It is from trees that we have created books which are stores of wisdom and have the ability to pass wisdom on, even through the ages. Our word 'book' and the German equivalent *Buch* derive from *boc* which technically referred not only to any kind of writing, but also to the beech tree as beech was often used as a material for writing and inscribing on. The French word for 'book', *livre* derives from the Latin *Librum* which originally referred to the inner bark of trees. The paper we use to create our writings, which for centuries allowed us to communicate with each other before the invention of the telephone or internet was, it turns out, created from a living being that was just as capable of communication as we are.

The more we learn about how trees communicate, the more we realise how complex and intelligent they are. Trees like other close-knit beings and eco-systems rely on each other to survive and thrive. Just as no human is an island, no tree is either. They rely on and support others as we do and are far more social and familial than was generally realised. The network by which trees communicate is called the Mycorrhizal network, but has been nicknamed the Wood Wide Web, a wordplay on how we humans now seem to communicate. This Wood Wide Web, like the World Wide Web, has fascinating parallels with the neurological pathways that exist within the human brain.

The Wood Wide Web is a complex and wonderfully labyrinthine underground system of roots and fungi via which trees communicate messages. All the trees in a woodland or forest are connected to this web, and to each other, in a symbiotic relationship with the fungi. This web is a support network that allows for communication and interaction between the trees and the fungi as well as providing a means by which nutrients, minerals, water, carbon and nitrogen is exchanged. This web allows them to survive, thrive and share information and resources between them.

Our brains and their Wood Wide Web function in a similar manner. Just as with our nervous systems, some of this communication between trees and fungi occurs through electrical pulses or chemical interactions. It turns out that trees can even give off what is essentially an urgent alarm call, by generating a particularly large electrical pulse which creates a crackling sound which is inaudible to us humans but very clearly noticed by other trees nearby. They can also issue warnings to each other by releasing chemicals into the air.

So, now that we know that trees can talk, what do they say to each other? Although modern science has yet to truly decipher this communication, it has been ascertained that trees do send signals and even warnings to each other about resources that they either need or have available for others, and about potential threats to them, such as insect infestations, drought and disease.

Trees can, and often will, change their behaviour based on the communications going on within the web, for example, to produce more chemicals that may deter certain bugs should a tree in the network inform them that those bugs have arrived in the forest.

What has been most fascinating about the discovery of the Wood Wide Web has been the revelation of the degree to which many of the trees and plants help each other out, and why they may be doing it. It turns out that parent trees can recognise their own offspring, those seeds which they produced that have since gone on to grow. Parent trees will prioritise and give more of their available resources and support to their own descendants than to others, although they are actually quite magnanimous and will still help others, just to a lesser degree than they help their own kin. Trees are not speciesist, trees of one species appear to gladly help those of other species. Evergreens and deciduous trees also seem to help each other out as needed through the seasons, depending on who is doing better and getting more natural resources at the time. So, it is all give and take. The trees appear to be happy to give to others because they seem to be aware that the others can and will help them when they need it. As a human, especially if you are quite a cynical soul, you may find yourself thinking 'but there is always one selfish soul, is there not?' Well, you are right. In the forest it is the Orchid; while they gladly take from the Wood Wide Web, they do not give anything back to it!

For many centuries many humans have been like the Orchid, always taking from the forest and the trees and never giving back. Hopefully now we can change that and become more like trees. We have much to offer them as they have much to offer us and there are many ways even in our everyday lives that we can help and support them, even if it is just choosing the recycled paper option or re-using a mug so we do not need yet another paper disposable one when we order a coffee. Be less Orchid, be more tree.

Given that trees are capable of communication with other trees and even fungi and that humans are also capable of communicating with other humans, and to some extent with other animals, suddenly it no longer seems such a crazy notion that perhaps humans and trees might also be able to communicate with each other...

Chapter 3

Ways to Connect with the Trees of the Ogham

Meditation Exercise

Please feel free to adapt this exercise to your personal needs and circumstances. It is here to inspire you and give you a few ideas.

Being out in nature reconnects us to Mother Earth and the energies of the other beings around us, including trees, plants and the earth. By connecting to these energies, we can help rebalance our own energies. We all have energies; each tree has its own energies and entire areas too, such as woodlands and forests, each have their own larger energies. Together, we are part of one great energy system encompassed by Mother Earth and Father Sky. Within natural, or even many managed environments, you can feel and sense the harmony of the energies and bring harmony to your own. You can even sense these energies from a very small pocket of nature, such as a lone tree or bush. Even the colours of nature are balanced – green, the colour of leaves and grass, is the balanced colour of the spectrum, while the browns of the trunks, fallen leaves and earth are formed from the three primary colours blended harmoniously together.

Trees are said to balance the three Celtic realms or elements of land, sea and sky, as indeed do we. These three elements are not abstract, they are very real, and all around and within us. Our physical form is one with the land, our blood and the water we drink is the sea, and the air that we breathe and the words through which we communicate represent the sky. By experiencing nature and reminding ourselves that we are a part of nature and that we, like nature, are the three realms or elements in balance, we can feel that great sense of oneness and connectedness.

By walking in the woods or sitting beneath a tree we are sharing energies and life force with that tree. It is the human/tree version of the sacred Māori *Hongi*, where two people touch nose and forehead and thereby share, exchange and intermingle the *ha* ('breath of life'). As with the *Hongi*, this is not a light undertaking and must be done seriously and with due respect and sense of sacredness. In this sharing two become one and it is the embracing of friendship, alliance, duties and responsibilities to the tree and to nature.

The meditation exercise below is not designed to be a one-off, it is designed to be performed over the long term, preferably on a regular or semi-regular basis as it is best to develop a meaningful and long-term relationship with the trees of the Ogham if you are serious about working with them. This exercise can be used with any and all of the trees covered in this book. Always approach trees and forests with respect, as though you were hoping to learn from or speak to a great mentor or elder.

Use your common sense when working with the trees or in parks or woodlands. Be safe and sensible – physically and spiritually. In the modern world we must take precautions to be safe. Take your mobile phone, take some food, drink and any medicines you need with you, let someone know where you are – or better still take someone with you. Create a safety checklist for yourself to work through if need be. There are some great ones available on various camping or hiking websites.

When working with the trees, use your natural instincts. If something does not feel right then do not force it. You can always try another tree or try again another time – like us they can have off-days or days when they need to be alone. Some trees may be very reticent to work with people because they are very aware of the immense harm that we have done to them over the centuries, others are far keener to work with us and are pleased to be approached. Do not give more of yourself or your time than you feel comfortable with. Always ask permission for your workings and await permission to be granted; do not proceed if it is not forthcoming.

Like us, trees like to be appreciated and cared for. It is all very well to thank the trees for their guidance, protection and wisdom, but to them the words of humankind do not mean a great deal, they prefer practical actions and emotional gratitude rather than just words. Some good ways of really showing your gratitude are to listen to what the tree asks you to do in exchange, to pick up litter from around the tree or whenever you see it, to offer it some water, offer it some love, become a volunteer ranger at a park, etc. If you are making offerings of water, please be aware that tap water is full of various chemicals such as fluoride, chlorine and lots of salts that can build up over time as many people find to their dismay when they come to repot a houseplant that has been watered with only tap water for months on end. As such, it can be harmful to the trees. A better way is to use collected rain water, such as from a water butt, or spring water. If tap water is your only option, leave it in the Sun for a few hours before offering it to the tree as this can help some of those chemicals to evaporate off.

If you are performing this meditation exercise in a public place, such as an open woodland, park or nature reserve, please do remain aware of your surroundings at all times. Do not close your eyes or drift away, just shift your awareness. Parks and woodlands are active places, with people and animals passing by so you need to be sensible – the last thing you want is to be communing with a tree and suddenly encounter an over friendly dog! If you have a group of friends who would also like to try this meditation, stay close together, around one or two trees. Appoint one person in the group to act as a watcher to be aware of what is going on around you while the rest of you can meditate at a deeper level. At home or in your garden you can, of course, go as deep as you like into meditation.

Do not worry if nothing much happens at first during your

meditation – these things take time and the trees are often very subtle. They are having to learn how to commune with us as much as we are having to learn how to commune with them, so be kind and patient. Pay attention to any feelings, memories, stories, impressions or images that come to you – these are messages for you. Also, pay attention to your dreams and discoveries for a few days, as messages may come to you that way. Record these things as well as any impressions and ideas in your journal or Book of Shadows. Sometimes things take on meaning over time and it is really handy to look back over what you have experienced.

If you live somewhere where it is difficult to find many trees or where the trees of the Ogham cannot readily be found, it is perfectly acceptable to work with photographs or even videos of the trees and woodlands. If you can get out into nature, into a woodland or park or even just your own yard while you do so can help to bridge the gap a bit. If you are limited to your own home or to a concrete jungle, then as well as working with photographs you may also like to add some nature into your space in the form of a few houseplants, some décor inspired by or created from nature, tree essences or essential oils.

Before meditation, magical workings or divination some people like to perform a protection exercise and to get themselves into the zone mentally and spiritually, and afterwards to perform a grounding exercise to bring them back to the everyday. The truth is though that we are spiritual beings and that nature and sacredness is all around us. It is just that sometimes it can do us good to set some boundaries and change our perspective for a while.

A popular method of protection is the bubble technique. Take a few relaxing breaths, slow and deep, until you feel calm and relaxed. Then visualise a pure divine light surrounding you, supporting you and enclosing you at a distance of around sixty centimetres all around, over your head and under your feet. The colour of the light is entirely up to you: some choose white or silver for its association with all things spiritual, some choose gold for that is a colour of power and the Sun, pink is also popular as it is a gentle, nurturing and loving colour, for working with the trees you could also try green as a colour of nature, love and balance.

Feel the sense of peace, love and the Divine within the bubble, protecting you. State an affirmation or prayer asking your Deity, or if you prefer a more general term try Spirit, grant you guidance, wisdom and protection during your work.

Afterwards you may like to ground yourself, though working with the trees is very grounding in itself. You can also perform this as part of your meditation exercise to better understand the nature of the tree with whom you are working. If you think about it, we too are very like trees. Stand or sit with your feet firmly on the floor, barefoot if possible. Relax, and see yourself growing roots, like a tree. Visualise the roots extending into the ground. Feel the energy of Mother Nature work its way up from the Earth, up your legs, up into your torso, along your arms, and up your neck into your head. Feel yourself filling up with the energy. When the energy has filled you up completely see it cascading from the top of your head and your hands, at the same rate that you are taking it up from your roots. See how your arms and head are like the branches of a tree and form a canopy. Imagine yourself as a tree or fountain of energy. This way you can benefit from the energy, and return it to the Earth. After a while imagine a light about thirty centimetres above your head. Visualise rays of light energy coming from above into the top of your head, down your body, and then entering the Earth via your roots.

To finish, visualise the light and your roots retracting a little and fading to your everyday sight, but know that they are always there at a lesser level for we are always connected to the Earth below and the Sky above us. Return your light energy bubble to where it came from or visualise it dissipating into the air, sending out positive energy to the world. When you are finished, thank the Universe, Stars, Earth or your Deity. Allow yourself to come back to the everyday on every level. Please do not do any strenuous activity, driving, or machine work until you have eaten and drunk something and feel fully back to normal. Write up your experiences as soon as you can afterwards, while they are still fresh in your mind and heart.

- Get to know a particular tree (or more if you like) of each of the twenty-five species linked with the Ogham Fews. It may be in a park, woodland or your garden. Do this exercise regularly throughout the year so you can get to know how the seasons affect the appearance and energy of the tree. It may take several sessions before the tree is willing to work with you. Do not worry if it takes a while, all friendships take time to build.

- Before you begin, set up your protective bubble to keep away any negative energies or to essentially cloak yourself from prying eyes if you are meditating in a public place.

- Be polite and introduce yourself to the tree. Ask for permission to work with it. Only proceed if given clear permission.

- Initially, sit a little way back from the tree, within its energy field, but far enough away that you can still see most of the tree if possible.

- Relax and just feel what it is like to be in the presence of such a tree. Listen to the sounds of the tree, the creaks in its boughs and the rustling noise of the leaves. In the ancient world trees were believed to speak to us through the rustling of their leaves.

- Smell the scent of the earth around you and of the tree. Notice if it is in bloom or fruiting. Smell the fragrance of the flowers or fruit. Watch the light play in the leaves.

- See how high its branches grow and imagine you can also see the roots mirroring that expanse within the earth.
- Take note of the physical form of the tree. Does it grow in the classic tree shape or is it short and shrubby? What form do the branches and leaves give its canopy? How tall is it? How mature is it? How large is its trunk?
- Study the forms and shapes of its bark. Is it smooth or deeply ridged?
- Observe its leaves, buds, blooms, fruit or nuts. Study their shape and form. Why have they evolved these features? Consider how these features grow and develop. What shape are the leaves? Are their edges smooth or serrated? Which colours can you see in the leaves? Although many trees have green leaves, their greens vary enormously. A great example is the Willow who has leaves that are different colours on both sides and whose green leaves have gorgeous tones of silver and blue as well as good old green.
- What are the key features that identify this tree and the season you are in? Over time, notice and embrace the small, subtle changes as the year turns and the tree matures.
- Look at the insects and animals that live within or on the tree. How does this tree provide for them? How does it cope, or not, with them living there?
- Allow yourself to just be with this tree. How do you feel in the presence of this tree? How does it feel in the presence of you?
- Be open to communicating with this tree. If you have anything to say to the tree, or any questions to ask, speak them either aloud or in your mind. As you get to know the spirit of the tree, you can move closer to the tree as

you work with it so that after a few sessions, and when it feels right for both you and the tree, you can sit with your back to the trunk of the tree, allowing your own trunk, roots and branches to merge temporarily with those of the tree during your time together. Enjoy the experience.

- Allow the tree to share its wisdom with you. See if you receive any messages from the tree. It can be in any form: perhaps a fallen leaf, a feather, a whisper in the wind, messages in the way the light is dappled by the leaves, or something you see in the leaves or pattern of the bark, a thought or memory that pops into your head, or a feeling in your heart.
- Perhaps you may wish to hug the tree, to share energies with it, if practical and the tree is willing – the thorny trees are by their nature not so huggable. Feel its great trunk in your arms, and touch its rough bark and leathery leaves. Be very gentle. Some parts of trees are toxic so always wash your hands afterwards, especially before eating or drinking anything.
- Ask if there is something the tree would like you to do for them. The tree may ask for some water, that you pick up some litter from by the trunk, that you plant a tree or that you try and use recycled paper. The trees will set you tasks to test you and see if they feel they can work with you.
- You may be given a gift from the tree, a fallen branch for a wand, or an acorn for a charm for example. Such tokens are traditionally carried as a talisman or amulet. Use these items to connect with the tree even when you are at home, to help you build up a long-term, mutual friendship.
- When you feel ready to leave, thank the spirit of the tree and leave an offering – one that is biodegradable and

sensitive to the tree's environment. Water that has been allowed to sit in the Sun or Moon and absorb some of that energy is always a welcome gift. If you do not have anything suitable with you, send your love, gratitude and blessings. It can be helpful to ground yourself afterwards.

- You may like to take photographs of this tree, through the different seasons and years so you can see how you both change over time. You could keep these photos in your magical journal or Book of Shadows. Make some space next to the photos so you can write down anything you have learned from that tree, any messages, dreams, wisdom or special moments you have shared. Such photographs can be very useful of for any reason you cannot commune with your special tree for a while.

- If you are feeling creative, you can also paint or draw the tree and whatever energies, vibe or wisdom it has. Share your creations with the tree on your next visit.

Other Ways to Connect to Trees and Forests

- As well as reading the information in this book, it is extremely important that you learn to understand your own very personal and magical relationship with the trees of the Ogham.

- Purchase a good tree identification guide, download an app or bookmark a good tree identification website. Look up the trees online and take a very good look at how they change through the seasons. Study their leaves, bark, catkins, flowers, or berries so that you can learn to identify them, whatever the time of year.

- Explore your personal memories and associations of the each of the twenty-five trees. Draw a spidergram or mind map listing ideas and thoughts that come to you about these trees.

- Take a walk in the woods or a stroll around town, you may be surprised how many of the different trees you can find in your neighbourhood.

- Take photographs of the trees, partly so you can learn to identify them, but also to allow you to connect with their energies on days when for whatever reason you cannot get out to spend time amongst them. This will help you to build up your knowledge of and connection to the trees. Photographs are also a good way to connect with and work with the trees if you live in a part of the world where they do not tend to grow.

- Pay attention to *The Celtic Tree Calendar*, see how the different trees and times of year affect you and your energies. Notice how the various trees and the forest changes as the months change. If you are in the Southern Hemisphere, you may like to flip the calendar by 180 degrees to better reflect your seasons.

- Plant a tree in your garden, and if practical, purchase it from a tree or woodland charity. If space is limited you could try growing Heather in a window box. Ivy can even be successfully grown as a houseplant. Tend the plant or tree as it grows. Let it speak to you of what it needs to grow and thrive.

- Have an image, carving, or photo of a tree (or trees) on your altar, in your personal space or even on a key fob, to remind you of their existence, energies, magic and wisdom as you go about your daily life.

- Carry one of the Staves with you each day or meditate on a Stave a day. See how the tree that Stave represents speaks to you throughout that day.

- Learn about the trees that exist or once existed in your local area. Are there any old tree tales from where you live? Are any of the roads, estates, farms, fields, etc named after trees? What grows well where you live? What does not grow so well?

- Research famous old trees from around the world, such as The Major Oak of Sherwood Forest (where Robin Hood is said by some to have hung out with his Merry Men), The Glastonbury Thorn with its mix of Pagan and Christian legends, The Fortingall Yew – reputed to be the oldest tree in the UK or Methuselah – the oldest living non-clonal tree in the world. What can their stories teach us?
- Are there any famous trees near you? What is their story?
- Keep up to date with any national and international *Tree of the Year* schemes to find out more about interesting or ancient trees around the globe.
- Join some interesting tree groups on social media, such as those on ancient trees, tree identification and working with trees.
- Research the fables, folklore, legends and deities associated with the trees of the Ogham or the Forests in general.
- Read poetry or prose or listen to music that is either about trees and woods, that has been inspired by them or that features them. Some good examples are *Why the Birch Tree Wears Slashes in its Bark, The Elder Mother* by Hans Christian Anderson, *The Oak* by Alfred Lord Tennyson or *The Lay of the Ash Tree* by Marie de France.
- Write your own poetry, prose and music about the trees and woodlands that inspire you or speak to you.
- Watch documentaries and YouTube videos on trees and woodlands.
- If you have wooden items at home, for example furniture, utensils or you live in a timber frame home, spend time studying its grain and colour. Thank the tree or trees that helped make it and take good care of it – give it a polish with natural products.
- You might like to try baking apple pie, making blackberry

jam or elderflower cordial, or otherwise consuming the edible gifts that the trees of the Ogham offer us. Be one hundred percent sure that what you are eating is safe and exactly what you think it is. Always give suitable thanks in exchange.

- You could also explore working with tree essences or essential oils derived from trees. Always endeavour to purchase from ethical and renewable sources.

- Make a biodegradable offering of Sun-water or something similar to local trees. Remember to give the trees and plants in your garden water and other nutrients they require to keep them happy and healthy. Same goes for your houseplants.

- Take some time to think of all the trees that humankind has felled. Consider how their felling has supported humankind's endeavours. Honour the trees that were sacrificed.

- Contemplate how the living forest supports others, above ground and below.

- Work with the trees and tree deities or saints associated with trees in your magical and spiritual practice. Ask the trees to bless your endeavours.

- Reflect on how you are like a tree in the forest. Which tree or trees are you most like? How do you change with the seasons? How have you matured and grown over time?

- Pay attention to your dreams. Do the trees speak to you in them? Research what dreaming of particular trees could mean.

- Volunteer or donate to a tree charity or engage with and support tree planting schemes. Adopt a tree. Next time you are shopping for presents, consider purchasing from a woodland or tree charity.

Part II

Chapter 4

The Ogham Set

Making an Ogham Set

You can purchase an Ogham set or you can make your own, it is entirely up to you. Either way make sure to really engage with them and dedicate them if you so wish. Traditionally to make your own Ogham set you would require a piece of wood from each of the twenty-five trees, but that is not necessarily practical and could take quite some time to collect, especially given the rarity these days of a few of the trees such as the Spindle or Wych Elm.

Making your own Ogham set requires dedication and time, but is an incredibly rewarding experience. By making your own set and putting your energy and intentions into it, you will be connecting more deeply and more personally to the set and to the trees that each Few represents. The effort, emotion and energy that you put into making your Ogham set helps to give it its energy; it is part of your offering in exchange for the wisdom of the Ogham and the forest. You will form a connection, completely unique to you, with your Ogham set and with the energies and forces that they represent. It is a deep and meaningful experience.

We know from legends and folklore that the Ogham and other magical symbols were originally carved on wooden Staves. Nowadays though Ogham sets are made of a wider range of materials such as clay, bone or stone as well as wood. Which material you use depends solely on your personal tastes, preferences and what you can get hold of. The key thing is to find/make a set that suits you. Whatever your Ogham Staves are made from, you will also need a drawstring bag or a piece of cloth to hold and store your cards or Staves in when not in use.

Stone / Crystal Set

Making an Ogham set from stones or crystals is probably the easiest method. Gather twenty-five stones or crystals of a similar shape and size and then paint the Fews onto them. As you paint each Few, chant its name and visualise the tree that it represents to empower it. Over time paint does chip from stones so you may wish to coat the symbol with some varnish. Clear nail varnish or craft varnishes work quite well.

If you choose to buy stones, for gemstones to make your set with, do check out bulk buy offers or bags of stones that some sellers offer on online marketplaces as it can help save you money. You can choose a gemstone that speaks to you, that represents something that it important to you, or is either your birthstone or is the crystal associated with the Tree that rules over the time you were born in *The Celtic Tree Calendar*.

Here are a few crystals with their traditional qualities:

Amethyst – Psychic development, spirituality and protection.
Aventurine – Health, luck and balance.
Carnelian – Energy, power and creativity.
Citrine – Prosperity, creativity and happiness.
Clear Quartz – Protection, energy and wisdom.
Haematite – Grounding, earthy and stone of the mind.
Howlite – Peace, harmony, psychism and communication.
Labradorite – Enlightenment, protection and revealing secrets.
Lapis Lazuli – Communication and wisdom.
Moonstone – Intuition, visions, psychism and magic.
Moss Agate – The natural world, especially plants and trees.
Red Jasper – Personal power, strength and energy.
Rose Quartz – Harmony, love and calm.
Snowflake Obsidian – Mysteries, optimism and balance.
Sodalite – Wisdom and spirituality.
Tiger Eye – Energy, the Sun and success.

Clay Set

You may like to create your own set from clay, especially if your connection with the element of earth is strong. Clay is easy to work with and allows you to be creative with the shapes of your Fews. Mould the clay into twenty-five versions of your desired shape. Carve in the Fews, chanting their names and envisioning their energy and associated tree as you do so and then fire them or allow them to dry, depending on the type of clay you are using.

Wooden Set

Wooden Staves are the traditional form. You may wish to work with the wood of a tree to whom you have a close connection, perhaps it is a tree you feel close to or that you have a lot in common with, perhaps it grows in your garden, or perhaps it is the tree that governs the time of year in which you were born. Of course, it could be a completely practical choice because you just happened to be gifted that piece of wood from that tree while you were out on a walk. It is also possible to make a set using the relevant wood for each of the trees, but getting a decent piece of Heather, Elecampane or Gorse for this can be very difficult.

Please do not cut twigs from living trees if you can possibly avoid it, instead collect fallen wood. The last thing you want to do when you are trying to build a positive new relationship with the trees or to build on an existing relationship with them is to go around hacking bits off them as that will only infuriate them.

Here are a few trees with their traditional qualities:

Apple – Health, magic and youth.
Ash – Associated with the world tree, balance and order.
Beech – Knowledge and wisdom.
Birch – Protection and fertility.
Cedar – Spirituality, preservation and prosperity.

Cherry – Happiness and love.

Elm – Health & magic.

Hazel – Wisdom and inspiration.

Holly – Protection and strength.

Maple – Luck and prosperity.

Oak – Tree of the Druids, strength and honour.

Olive – Peace, healing and spirituality.

Peach – Youth, fertility and health.

Pine – Protection, purification and prosperity.

Rowan – Magic and inspiration.

Yew – Associated with renewal and divination.

Round Branch Cut Staves

Find a branch that has a diameter of about two-and-a-half centimetres as this will give you a nice sized roughly circular disk to work with. Some people like to remove the bark, this can be done with a knife, or you may prefer to leave the bark on for a more natural look – the choice is yours. Wrap some cloth around the branch before it goes in the vice though to avoid the teeth marking the wood. Saw the Branch into twenty-five pieces using a hacksaw and place it in a vice to hold it steady. The disks can be sanded down to a smooth finish or left rough and rustic.

Twig Cut Staves

Find a branch or a thickish twig, that is about one to two centimetres wide and cut into sections. Leave the bark on for the moment. Now some people like their twig style Staves to be shorter say about five to six centimetres while others prefer them longer to about ten to twelve centimetres. Go with what works for you and how big or small your hands are as you will want to be comfortable handling them. Then remove a section of the bark in the middle of the new Few. You can either just take a small section out, large enough for just the symbol of the Few or you can take a longer strip and write not only the Few's symbol but also its name in either or both the Gaelic and English, depending on your personal preference.

Square or Rectangular Cut Staves

If you have access to reclaimed wood or cut-offs you may prefer rectangular or square Staves. Simply cut up your piece of wood into twenty-five square or rectangular pieces. Try to sand the edges down to get a smooth finish though as this will make the staves more pleasant to handle.

Whichever method you have gone for, when it comes to marking the Few itself, you have a choice of whether to carve it into the wood, paint it on the wood or burn it into the wood with a pyrography tool. It is always worth practising this out on a spare piece of the wood first to be sure that you can get the effect that you are after. For example, some paints may leach into the wood leaving a rather messy look, in which case seal the wood first and paint over the sealant then seal again.

If you wish to read using reversed meanings, place a dot beneath the Few symbol, so you will be able to tell if you have cast it upright or reversed.

As you carve or paint each Few, chant its name to empower it and visualise the relevant tree in all its natural and beautiful glory.

When you are happy with your set you may like to seal or varnish them. It is best to use a natural varnish or sealant that while protecting the wood will still let it breathe.

Ogham Cards

These are not ideal for Ogham divination as they cannot be cast so easily; they also tend to get tatty very quickly when frequently handled. Ogham Cards are great though for meditation work and while learning them or seeing if the Ogham is for you before investing the time and money in getting/making a set. You will need to cut up card into twenty-five pieces or purchase a set of cards, such as index cards. The size of card you choose will depend entirely on the size of your hands. You want to be able to comfortably handle and shuffle them. For a person with average size hands about eight centimetres by twelve centimetres is a nice, practical size. On the front of the card, you could draw or paint the Few in the centre of the card and perhaps write one or two keywords relating to it around it. You could also get creative with your computer and then print out your designs onto card, which you then cut up. That way when your set does get tatty and in need of replacing, you can recycle the old set and print out a new one. There are also some lovely commercial card sets out there, if that is more your thing.

Consecrating, Empowering and Cleansing and Refreshing their Energies

Consecration completes the process of making your own set, it fills them with energy and makes them ready and fit for usage. You may wish to consecrate each Stave separately, or the whole set at once. You may wish to dedicate your Ogham set, perhaps to a particular God or Goddess that you work with, to the trees of the forest, or to something that you want to achieve with them such as understanding of the great mysteries, to inner peace, etc. How you consecrate your staves is up to you and your practice, but many beginners like to consecrate them with the four five elements: passing the Staves above a flame for fire, through the smoke of an incense stick for air, placing them is some salt or soil for earth, dipping their tip in a bowl of water for water and breathing on them for spirit.

We empower our Ogham set by putting energy into them, such as chanting their names as we carve or paint the Fews, we also empower them, and ourselves, through working with them.

As you use and work with your Staves, they will pick up energies over time. Not all of these energies are good and their own positive energies may fade. So, every so often, it is always worth cleansing any negative or stagnant energies from your set and re-invigorating them with some fresh energy to keep them content and working well. You will know when your set needs cleansing because it may feel tired, yucky or become very vague or hollow in the readings that it gives you.

How you cleanse and refresh your Ogham set will depend on what they are made of. Some like to cleanse and refresh the energies of their set under the Moon at the time of the Full Moon, others prefer to cleanse and empower them with the light of the Sun. Another method is to pass each Stave through the smoke of an incense stick while visualising them being cleansed, cleared of negative energies and re-invigorated. One method that works really well, especially with wooden Staves, is to take your Staves with you on a walk on the woods or out in nature. Find a quiet spot and get your Staves out. Place them at the base of a tree and sit down with them. Ask the forest and the tree to cleanse and rejuvenate their energies. You too can benefit from this, ask the tree or forest to do the same for you too and spend some time getting to know the trees and the forest around you. When you are done, pack up your Ogham set and leave a suitable biodegradable offering as thanks.

Chapter 5

Divining with the Ogham

Did the Druids and the Celts use Ogham for Divination?

In ancient times a lot of cultures actively practised divination of various kinds. Unfortunately, the ancient Druids and Celts did not leave much written information behind. Instead, we have to rely on what the Roman writers of the time had to say about the Druids and divination; their information often came second hand and with a whole lot of prejudice. The Romans do make it clear that among the many roles performed by the Druids, they were Prophets or *Fáith* who performed augury and divination. They did this for many varied reasons, such as to discover lucky or unlucky days to do certain things or to predict the outcome of a battle. There were many methods of augury and divination that the Druids made use of. They would study the flight and the calls of birds, the patterns of the clouds and even study the entrails of sacrificed animals. It was even recorded that the infamous Iceni Queen, Boudicca, used the running of a hare to predict the outcome of what was to be her last great battle against the Romans.[11] Boudicca predicted based on the way the hare ran, that the Romans too would soon be fleeing, but this was not the case.

One of the problems is that even if our Celtic forebears were practicing divination with Ogham Staves, such Staves, being of wood, would be very unlikely to last to the present day for wood degrades over time. Ancient wooden artefacts are a rare find and only possible thanks to certain conditions, such as being immersed in a bog for hundreds of years which stops certain processed from breaking down the wood. One artefact that has survived, that possibly alludes to the use of Ogham or wooden Staves for divination, is the Coligny Calendar. The

Coligny Calendar is a bronze tablet that dates back to the second century CE and within the calendar there are several days marked with *Prinni Louden* which means 'the Casting of Woods' and *Prinni Layet* meaning 'the 'Laying of Woods'. Perhaps the days marked with these terms were considered to be good days for divination?

We can also gleam information on any Celtic divinatory practices from legends and folklore. The Goddess and Saint Brighid is credited with creating a form of augury that involves 'seeing' through hands curled into the classic 'telescope' form and folklore tells us that people believed that you could divine the future by staring through a holed stone.

In the hagiography of St Patrick, the fifth-century CE Patron Saint of Ireland, we find reference to a form of divination called the Swimming of Names. Names or letters to represent specific things or people were carved upon Birch bark – just as the first Ogham was said to be – and placed in a bowl of water. Those that sank were deemed unlucky or not relevant to events, while those that floated were considered lucky or relevant.

In the Irish tale, *Tochmarc Étaíne* or *'The Wooing of Etain'*, which dates as back at least as far as the twelfth century CE, a Druid named Dalan is described as using a method of Ogham divination to find where the God Midir had taken Etain.[12] It is said that Dalan cut four wands of Yew on which he inscribed three Oghams, and used them to find the keys of divination, which enabled him to discover that she had been taken to the fairy mound of Breg Leith, where Midir dwelt.

According to *The Tale of Taliesin*, recorded in the Welsh collection of Legends known as *The Mabinogion*, the great Bard and Druid, Taliesin, who was reborn from the Goddess Ceridwen, practised a form of divination that appears to use sprigs or Staves, which could well be Ogham Staves. In one of his poems, he states:

'I am Taliesin,
Chief of the Bards of the West,
I am acquainted with every sprig/stave
In the cave of the Arch-Diviner'.[13]

In *The Scholar's Primer*, there is listed a divination technique using the Ogham for divining the sex of an unborn child. If this is the first child of the Mother-to-be, you look at her name and transcribe it into the letters of the Ogham (and remember the Ogham letters can represent multiple Latin letters). If it has an even number of letters, it portends that the child will be a girl, if it has an odd number of letters, the child will be a boy. If the Mother-to-be has already born a child, you use the name of her last child instead of her name.[14] If the Ogham was used for this form of divination, was it used for others too in the past?

The sources that we have for the Ogham all seem to imply that there is much more to the Ogham Fews than simply representing a sound or letter. The kennings of *The Word Oghams*, *The Ogham Tract* and the glosses of *The Scholar's Primer* all provide a way for us to interpret the meanings of the Fews for divination, whether or not that was their original intention.

The very shape of the Ogham Fews appear to suggest that it was not meant for normal, secular, everyday use. While Ogham is a great way to inscribe a short memorial or message on a standing stone or piece of wood, it is a very impractical system for writing anything longer, which is why it is believed by so many that the Ogham contained hidden secrets for divination that could only be understood by the initiated.

The problem with Ogham divination is that we do not know the details of how it was done in the past for the most part, the Druid's have left very few – if any – clues, their methods were shrouded in secrecy, told only to the initiated. This is why those of us who seek to work with and divine with the Ogham have had to get creative. I would also strongly encourage you to get creative too, it will deepen your connection with and understanding of the Ogham.

How Does Divination Work?

According to the analytical psychologist Carl Jung, it is all down to something called synchronicity. Synchronicity means things happening together in time. It is those strange, unexplained coincidences that we have all experienced, such as when we find ourselves thinking of a friend, then seconds or minutes later, they give us a phone call or we bump into them. Jung used synchronicity to refer to circumstances that appear meaningfully related and fully acknowledged that the meaning that we give to such coincidences comes from within us. The human brain loves to make connections between things and to see patterns, it is ultimately what it has evolved to do. This is how we know what poses a danger to us, and what foods are safe or unsafe to eat. It is also how we make our lives a meaningful experience.

The meaning that we give to coincidences connects both the outer world and our own inner world. For example, when we smell certain scents around us, we may recall certain memories or emotions completely unbidden by our conscious brain. The memory has arisen from our subconscious prompted by the scent. Through ascribing meaning to things such as coincidences we can connect our subconscious and conscious mind, and our own mind to the greater collective unconscious. The collective unconscious is supposed to explain why all over the world, in very different cultures, we can find symbols that seem to have very similar meanings or associations.

It is through symbolism, experience, knowledge and coincidences that we give meaning to the Ogham, the Runes, the I-Ching, the Tarot and even road signs. Each symbol is a key that gives us access to so much more that lies behind it, for it has a meaning far greater than itself. This is what makes divination possible.

Divination allows you to clear through the clutter of your chattering confused mind to reveal your inner thoughts and feelings. It provides a means of focus and can be a very valuable bit of me time to allow you to discover and process what is going on with you at any time.

Divination is an art; it is a way of revealing hidden or unknown insights into the subtle energies of the movements, patterns and paths in one's life. It is not something to take lightly or to view as a joke. It takes work, patience, a deep understanding of the energies you are working with and a deep understanding of yourself.

Divination is not fortune telling, rather it is more like being a meteorologist who predicts the weather by studying weather maps. Like the meteorologist, we use symbolism, patterns, experience and knowledge of the situation to guide us into coming up with a plan or prediction.

Divination involves reading the signs and symbols around us, but also to examine what is going on inside of us and to connect the two. The Ogham, like any form of divination, serves as an external prompt or set of symbols that we can use to explore what is going on for us, our thoughts, emotions and our circumstances. We create the link between the stave or staves that we pull and what is going on in our lives. For example, if you cast the Willow in a reading, it can mean many things, such as sadness, healing, magic and more. At that moment what you see in the Willow at any one time reflects your inner thoughts and feelings. If you pull the same Willow stave tomorrow it could mean something entirely different to you than it does today.

Divination illustrates the issue or situation at hand and our own feelings and thoughts. It can illuminate what had led us to this situation, what caused it, what is going on at the present time and guide us as to what is the next logical step or probable outcome. Any outcome is not set in stone; we have the power to make changes if we so wish.

Performing Divination

As with the meditation exercise, some people like to perform a short protection exercise prior to reading and to ground themselves afterwards. You can use the exercises given in Chapter 3.

You may also like to say a prayer or blessing as you settle down to perform divination, to open yourself to the messages you are about to receive and to ask for protection and guidance. Here for inspiration is a charm that I like to recite:

> *'Spirits of the Trees*
> *Reveal to me the mysteries.*
> *Please bless these staves*
> *so I may see the waves*
> *and patterns in the energies.*
> *Blessings and thanks to you my friends*
> *Who guard and guide me to the end.'*

As well as the traditional meaning I have given for each of the Staves and Fews that follows, you will have and develop your own understanding of what each Few means to you. Incorporate your own ideas and research into how you work with the Ogham wherever possible as it will make it so much more meaningful for you.

Be aware of each Few and what it represents, and remember each Few has a tree, bird, river, colours and so much more associated with it. Each Few will inspire sensations, phrases, words, feelings, ideas, connections, thoughts, memories, images or some other kind of association to surface up from deep within you as you work with them or perform a divinatory reading. This is a perfectly natural part of the process. Allow the Ogham to speak to you in this very personal way and pay close attention to these messages.

Performing divinatory readings for yourself is the best

way to learn. Keep a diary or journal and make notes on your readings, you can then go back to them and see how accurate (or not) you were. This will help you to develop your divinatory skills. Do not read for others, even for friends, until you have a great deal of experience behind you, because when we perform readings, we ultimately are giving our own personal opinion on events and it takes a great deal of experience and training to move beyond that.

Divination works best when you need to contemplate or seek guidance for specific issues and situations, for example finding out how you really feel about a situation, or what to do in a specific situation, what you need to do to ensure the success of a project or if you want to get a good overview of the major factors that may come into play in say, the next year. The Ogham shows you what is what and can help you to formulate your own guidance and decisions as to what you want to do next. It never tells us what to do, but always leaves that part very much in our hands. It can also be very rewarding to choose a Stave for the day and to see how that Stave, and what it represents, speaks to you during that day, this is also one of the best ways to truly learn what each Stave and tree means to you.

To accurately perform divination, you need to respect and understand the system with which you are working and to be aware that you will be opening yourself up, mentally and spiritually to the energies you are working with. This is why in this book I have tried to give you an understanding of the cultural and spiritual background to the Ogham and the trees that are associated with it. I would also strongly urge to learn more as you deepen your divination practice.

First of all, ask yourself are you in the right mood to perform divination? If you are stressed, antsy, tired, confused, overly emotional, busy or just in the right frame of mind, do not do it, you will not get a decent reading out of it. Instead, either wait until you are in the right frame of mind or do what you need to do to get yourself there.

If possible, create the right environment prior to undertaking a divinatory reading so that you can truly and calmly focus upon it and better explore what is presented before you and examine your own thoughts and ideas about it. So, get any distractions out of the way and turn off your phone. You may like to burn some incense or an aromatherapy candle, or meditate to get you into a suitable frame of mind.

Consider carefully what you are consulting the Ogham for. Prior to any reading you need to mediate on the issue or question that you are seeking advice on, even if only for a few moments. What is it that you hope to gain from the session? What is it that you are seeking to know or to find? Where is this desire coming from? Is it a question born of your spirit, your mind or your heart? If you have a question in mind, formulate it very carefully so that it actually asks exactly what you are wishing to learn, otherwise your reading can be vague or answer a completely different question for you. Keep it focused and make it clear. Always beware the self-fulfilling prophecy or of seeking confirmation for what you have already decided to do. Be specific if you can with what it is you are seeking, otherwise it is perfectly acceptable to ask for generic guidance from the Ogham and the trees. Many people will simply ask for guidance and advice for the next day, week or year ahead and then let the Ogham talk to them.

Consider which spread or divination method you wish to use. Which one will work best for what you want to ask? Sometimes, something will happen and you will end up doing a completely different spread to the one you intended. Do not worry and go with it, the Ogham is trying to tell you something, so it is best to listen.

You may prefer to just state the question clearly. Then shuffle the Staves and draw out the required number. Either cast them or spread them out as per the method you have chosen. If any additional Staves jump out when you are drawing them, just add them to your reading – they obviously have something important to convey to you.

Begin by taking some time to just look at the way the Staves have fallen or been laid out. Open yourself to any images, thoughts or emotions that you get. What is your initial impression? How does the spread look to you? What strikes you as obvious? Note whether the Stave is upright or reversed and how close together or far apart they are. Staves that appear close together are more closely connected than those which are further apart.

Take a quick look at the Staves before you and consider first just the key words and impressions that they give you. How do they relate to each other? Are their messages similar or contradictory? Are the trees that the Staves represent similar or different? For example, if you have cast trees that are all thorny, evergreen or in the Rose family what may that be suggesting to you?

Next take a closer look at each of the Staves, how it has fallen or where it is laid. Consider the meaning of each of the Staves, both in terms of the text of this book and what it means to you. How does each Stave contribute to answering your question? What guidance or wisdom does it offer to you? At this point you may like to imagine yourself as literally communing with the tree that the Stave represents and allowing it to talk to you. Imagine you are there with the tree, listening to the messages it whispers as its leaves move in the wind. Imagine it showing you images and symbols via the way its leaves play with light and shadow. Let it speak to you, spirit to spirit. Let it be a magical and spiritual experience rather than just staring at a symbol carved on a bit of wood.

What themes can you see laid out before you? How do the Staves and the trees they represent relate to each other? What do they have in common? For example, are they all to do with healing, magic or the cycle of life? How are they different? This is where psychic intuition and the brain's natural desire to see patterns in everything comes in. Do not overcomplicate it and just go with what flows into your mind and heart. Read it as though it were a story, the story of your life at the current time. This is why divination is an art, and needs practice.

Consider how the reading before you relates to your original question or intention? What are those themes that you have uncovered telling you about what is going on within you and within your life? Can you see yourself in the story that the Staves are telling you?

I would recommend gradually introducing more depth to your readings as you gain experience and confidence. For your first few readings focus on what the Few means to you, the keywords, *The Word Ogham* Kennings and the associated tree. Gradually build on this as you get to know the trees, their legends and lore better and bring in more of the full explanation for each Few as well as anything you have learned from your own research. Once you feel confident that you have a good understanding of all that, you can then add in what each Few represents in more and more of the other Oghams, such as the bird it represents, its colour or the number and type of people it depicts according to the People Ogham. The full list of the different types of Ogham can be found in *The Ogham Tract*. I've included a link to an online translation of this text in the Websites section at the end of this book.

Spreads and Methods

In this part of the book, I will provide various different divination spreads, some are older, some are pretty modern and a couple are borrowed from other divination methods. This does not detract from their effectiveness. Experiment and find which spreads work best for you. You can also design your own by drawing on the world around you, the trees, Celtic legends, folklore and personal experience. Work with the Ogham and its trees, and let them work with you. Allow your own relationship with the Ogham to guide you.

The Single Stave Method

This is a quick reading, good for dealing with a specific problem. Read it in relation to the question you have posed or what is on your mind at the moment. This is sometimes used for yes / no answers: right way up is yes and reversed is no. Many people will also use this method each morning to select a Stave to guide and inspire them for the day ahead, which is a great way to get to know what each Stave means for you.

The Three Staves Spread

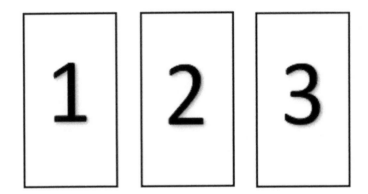

This is great for quite specific questions or to get a mini-overview of a situation. Draw three Staves and place them as shown. The Staves should be read from left to right, as the Ogham is. The first Stave relates to the cause of the problem or the past, the second is the present or the current situation, the third Stave is the possible outcome of the situation or the future.

The Three Realms Spread

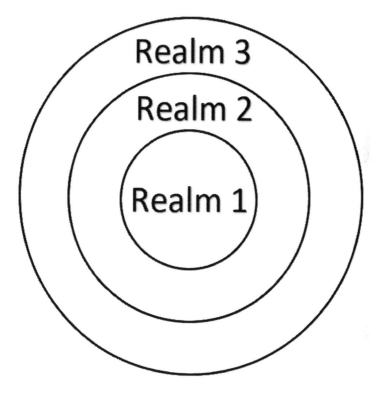

According to Celtic Tradition, things often come in threes. For the Celts there were three realms of existence and three elements: Land, Sea and Sky. Draw out three concentric circles on a cloth or piece of paper. Decide what these three circles represent. They could be Land, Sea and Sky as a three element spread. You could assign them to be Past, Present and Future. Or you could have them represent the Ancestors, the Spirits of Nature and the Gods, especially if you are using the Ogham to gain guidance and wisdom from these wise ones. Toss a set number of Staves into the air and interpret them based on which realm they land in.

The Four Directions or Four Elements Method

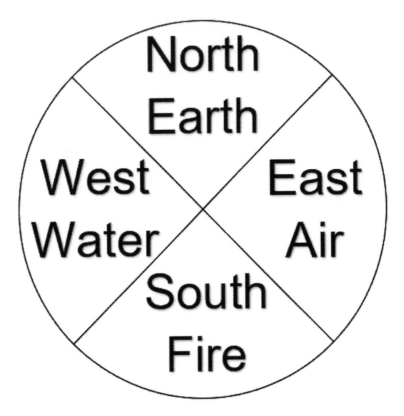

This method needs a cloth or piece of paper marked with the four quarters. You will also need a compass if you wish to line it up correctly with the cardinal directions as you cast.

Select four Staves at random. Place the first in the North, the second in the East, the third in the South and the fourth in the West. Alternatively, you may like to select four Staves and then cast them randomly onto the cloth or paper. It can be very revealing how they fall.

North represents Earth and relates to stability, security, solidity, stillness, the practical, fertility and regeneration.

East is Air and relates to victory, survival, feelings, communication, movement, the intellect and logic.

South is Fire and relates to inspiration, change, initiative, enterprise, passion, get up and go, and leadership.

West is Water and relates to truth, knowledge, wisdom, emotions, intuition, dreams and cleansing.

Sample Reading

This is a reading conducted for a friend of mine who was about to start a new job. The new job was in a call centre whereas her previous job had been a secretary. She was terrified that she would not fit in to the new, busier environment. The spread showed Duir in the North, Ngeadal in East, Ur in South and Luis in West.

The main theme here is change, of situation, the need to change, etc.

Duir / Oak in North – The new job will bring great stability and protection into your life. Your home and finances are about to become more secure.

Ngeadal / Broom in air – Shows the need to clear away old patterns of thought and old feelings to be able to fully embrace and make the most of this change. Your routine and outlook will undergo a large change with this new job, but it will feel like a positive one.

Ur / Heather in fire – You seem to be passionate about the new job, and you are able to pass that enthusiasm and passion to others. You will enjoy it.

Luis / Rowan in water – Discover what inspires your creativity you and seek out those forces. Follow your dreams and intuition. In your new place of work, and in your life as a whole, surround yourself with the people who inspire you, who bring you out of your shell and who make you feel as if you can achieve your goals.

The Four Elements method can also work well if you add a fifth element, that of Akasha or spirit. So, Staves that fall in the centre represents spiritual influences and the Divine.

The Tree Spread

Useful when you are at a crossroads in your life, could be spiritual, emotional, or even relating to your career. Can also be used when you know the way forward, but need some advice. Lay out 4 Staves as below:

1   is your current position.
2   shows factors that will assist you on your path.

4   shows factors that will hinder you.
3   represents the most likely outcome, or the best path
     forward.

The Five Keys Method

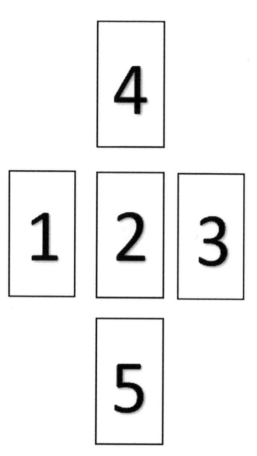

The Five Keys reading is used to plot the arc of your life, and the forces influencing it. It gives quite a comprehensive overview of the situation and is also a good spread for helping with business decisions. Lay out five Staves in the form of a cross. Read the Staves in the order of 2 1 4 5 3

2 represents the present position/situation and your current state of mind about the issue.

1 shows the events leading up to, and possibly causing the current situation of Stave 2.

4 shows help that you are likely to get, in the near future and where that help will come from.

5 represents aspects of the situation that is set in place by fate.

3 is the critical element of the future, showing future influences on the situation, the solution and the probable outcome.

The Celtic Cross Spread

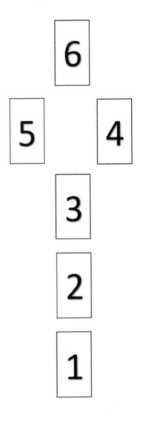

This is useful if you are really unsure about a situation or issue as it reflects the issue back to you.

1   shows the root of your confusion.
2   shows where you need to be focusing your energies and the direction to take.
3   shows elements or obstacles in your way.
4   tells you what will help you to overcome the obstacles that were revealed by Stave 3.
5   will point to what else you are lacking at the moment.
6   Is the probable outcome of the situation or experience.

Ceridwen's Cauldron Spread

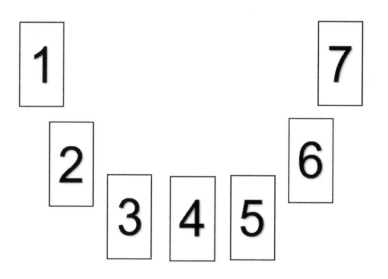

This is good for when you need a little bit of help in your way forward or a little drop of inspiration, after all the Ancient Welsh Goddess Ceridwen was the keeper of the Cauldron of Inspiration.

1   shows aspects of the past influencing the situation.

2   shows aspects of the present influencing the situation.

3   this shows future aspects influencing the situation.

4   is the centre of the spread, and tells you the best route to take towards a successful outcome, and to get out of the cauldron.

5   suggests the attitudes of others to you, if you follow the path set out by Stave 4.

6   as you start to climb up out of the cauldron, which is not easy; here we find the obstacles or issues blocking your path.

7   is the most probable outcome for the situation.

Sample Reading

Mandy is in the process of moving out from being with her parents and in with her boyfriend. She is still quite young, and is quite worried about the whole situation. She feels moving in with her love is right, but feels terribly guilty about leaving her parents. Mandy needs a bit of inspiration. The reading clearly shows the ending of one part of her life and the beginning of something new.

1   Nuinn / Ash is the past, signifying her growing up with her parents, it also shows that she has a harmonious and healthy relationship with them. Also shows the order of things and that it is inevitable that Mandy will have to move out at some point.

2   Ruis / Elder is the present, showing her transformation as she moves out and sets up home with her partner. Mandy will experience some sadness in the process, but this Few also shows the inevitability that she cannot live with her parents for the rest of her life. Elder gives an opportunity to Mandy's parents for a new start as much as it does to Mandy.

3   Eamhancholl / Wych Elm is the future aspect, and Wych

Elm is all about transitioning and cycling through life's stages. All the signs and omens are indicating that this is a good move and the right time to undertake it. It is a natural transition, a natural step in Mandy's life path and that of her partner, and it all feels very much like it is just meant to be.

4   Tinne / Holly is the crux, advising the best course of action to achieve the best outcome. Here holly emphasises the need for patience with everyone involved, there will be a period of adjustment where everyone will have to learn to get on with and adapt to the new situation. It may feel like a challenge but everyone, and especially Mandy's relationship with her partner will become stronger as a result.

5   Onn / Gorse encourages her to take the plunge and shows that this is a great opportunity and blessing for Mandy and her partner. It suggests that others around her will be happy for her, and they are optimistic about her new relationship. Crucially for Mandy it shows that her parents as well as her partner will be there for her through this change.

6   Ailm / Pine is the obstacle, and is reversed. Mandy feels as if someone has stopped listening to her when she talks about the move. Perhaps that person has switched off because Mandy keeps talking about moving out, but has not actually done so yet. Here Ailm is sort of telling her to get on with the move, to stop talking and start doing.

7   Ngeadal / Broom is the probable outcome, it shows that Mandy is very likely to move in with her partner and in doing so she will have a sort of Spring clean within her life – it will pave the way for her future. It is a time to take stock, and here says that Mandy is going to have to learn to look after and rely on herself, rather than relying

on her parents. She will also have to learn to adapt to living with her partner and together they can and will forge a strong, healthy and happy home.

The Wheel of the Year

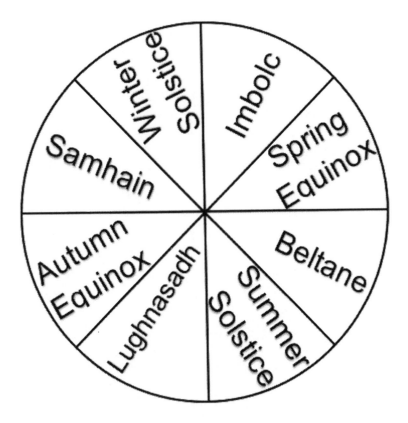

The Modern Pagan Year is based on an eight spoked wheel, with each spoke representing one of the eight major Sabbats. To use this method, you may need to read up on the four Festivals of the Celtic year, the two Equinoxes and the two Solstices. Alternatively, you can substitute the eight spoked wheel of the year with the four seasons. This spread is used to give you an overview of the year ahead, to show you longer term themes and patterns. Pick out eight Fews and lay them out as one per Festival.

Random Casting Method

This is based on a method called 'Riding the Wagon' where Runes are cast, we are just using the Ogham instead. Sit down on the floor. First select how many Staves you wish to cast. Then cast them randomly in front of you. Those that land nearer you are the Staves that represent the past, the middle ones are more present issues and those that land further away represent matters that are further in the future. The Staves that land to your left represent your personal, internal issues that are influencing external events, while those that land on the right are the outside factors and events influencing you.

The Astrological Method

This is a modern method, based on the twelve astrological houses. It works well, and is useful for getting a clear picture of your (or your client's) life. How close the Fews land to the centre is relevant, closer to the centre indicates the issues of the present, while those further away are further into the future. You will need a cloth or large piece of paper marked out with the 12 houses.

House 1 at the nine o'clock position is the house relating to the Self. It shows the sum total of your being, your personality, the approach to life, inner and outer health, state of mind, actions, your essential qualities and what motivates you.

House 2 at eight o'clock is the house of finance, money and material possessions. Shows your attitudes to partnerships, and business. Interestingly this is also the house of self-esteem. When you think about it, it is true that what you have is often a big part of your self-esteem. Much of what we own is chosen to make us feel better about ourselves.

House 3 at seven o'clock is the house of communication, much of this communication is that between you and those you hold close, such as family and friends. It relates to education and intelligence, short journeys and the environment. It is about harnessing intelligence to share it effectively with others.

House 4 at six o'clock is the house of family and home. We create homes as sanctuaries, somewhere to physically and psychologically come home to, for our family and ourselves. Herein lies domesticity, ancestry, roots and heritage. This is also the house of the Mother or the Nurturer.

House 5 at five o'clock is the house of pleasure and creativity. This is about procreation and children, but also the creation of art and the enjoyment of culture and the arts, emotional enrichment, and affairs of the heart. Your parent's influence on your life appears here as we are creations of and often a sort of extension of our parents.

House 6 at four o'clock relates to your personal well-being and how you look after yourself. The sixth house indicates where physical problems may require adjustment in the form of exercise, diet or medical treatment. Any Staves here show that health is a key factor at this time.

House 7 at three o'clock is the house of your commitment to others. This house concerns all direct close personal relationships with others and reveals the nature of other people's reactions to our actions. It rules marriage, partnerships, close personal friendships and contact with people in general. The Seventh House is closely related to the workings of karma.

House 8 at two o'clock relates to sexuality, self-awareness, inherited finance and sometimes deceit. The eighth house is a rich source of information about areas of life that we tend to examine only when we are forced to by circumstances and other people.

House 9 at one o'clock is the house of philosophy. It is the house relating to your search for meaning to life and your ideology. It relates to life as a voyage of discovery and by association to foreign journeys too. It shows spiritual and psychic development.

House 10 at twelve o'clock is the house of status. It is about the place you have attained in your career, group and society. Fame, desires, goals, ambition and achievement are all shown here. House 10 relates to your dealing with authority and superiors. House 10 is also the house of the Father or the more authoritarian parent.

House 11 at eleven o'clock is where elements of your social life appear. It also shows your attitude to social responsibility. Circumstances beyond your control are also reflected in the Eleventh House.

House 12 at ten o'clock. Private matters are displayed in the Twelfth House, such as faith, enlightenment and your personal attitude to others. Psychic and intuitive processes also shown here.

Fionn's Window or Ridge Pole

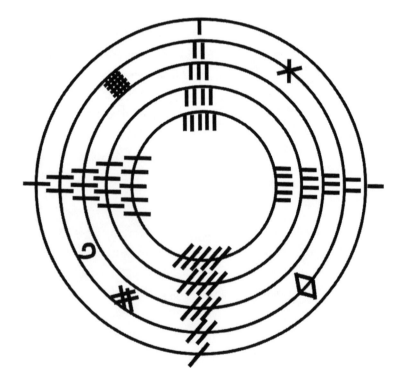

This version utilises the *Fege Find* which translates as 'Fionn's

Window' or 'Fionn's Ridge Pole', also known as the Wheel Ogham of Choicest rhetoric, which is the map of the Ogham Fews from *The Book of Ballymote*. It was named after Fionn mac Cumhaill, the Irish Hero and Giant who is credited with achieving many great feats and even with building the Giant's Causeway in Country Antrim.

As the ridge pole it is said to represent the main pole that held up an Iron Age round house, the Druim or line which the Ogham is written on, a tree trunk or even the World Tree or World Pillar. As the window it is reputed to allow us, like all windows do, to see into and through the mysteries of the Ogham. To say this image is cryptic is an understatement! It seems to be a tool for Ogham working. Some claim to have deciphered it, what do you think?

Feel free to create your own ways of working with this window. This method is ideal for beginners or if you have not completed the process of making or getting hold of your own Ogham set yet. First create your window, either photocopy and enlarge the version here or create your own. Next take a marker and allow it to randomly drop onto the wheel. Your chosen Few is the one closest to where the stone lands. You can cast your stone as often as you like to give you the Fews you need to make up your reading.

You can use multiple markers as well and decide in advance what each marker will represent. For example:

- If you were asking about personal dynamic between two people you may cast a marker for each person, and maybe another one for external factors or the issue itself.
- For a past, present, future reading you would cast a marker for each.
- For an elements reading you would have a marker for each element. If you wish to stick to the traditional Celtic elements of Land, Sea and Sky.

- A mind, body and soul reading would require three markers, one for each aspect.
- Those of you who are confident with the astrological method may like to cast a marker for each House, or have markers to represent planets and their influences with another marker to represent the person asking the question.

There is also no reason why you cannot cast your Ogham Staves onto Fionn's Window; you interpret the Staves as usual but also tie them in with the Few that each lands near on the chart. You may like to think of each area or zone on the chart as being ruled by the Few shown there, and that area being the House of that Few. For example, if the Stave of Fearn lands near the Beith Few marked on the chart, it may highlight the need to seek guidance about or perhaps to make a compromise over a new project or changes occurring at that time. If a Few lands across two Fews as marked on the chart, interpret it in relation to both.

Part III

Chapter 6

The Format

In the following chapters we will be looking at each Few in detail, their correspondences, meaning, mythology, folklore and more. We begin with the name of the Few and the tree is has become associated with, followed by – where known – the original meaning. This is to give you a better understanding of how the meaning has changed and allows you to explore each Few and its meaning more deeply if you so wish. The keywords are there in case you just want the basics of the meaning of the Few, kind of like a quick reference, and you will also find a handy quick reference guide at the back of this book so you can avoid flicking through the whole thing when you just want to be reminded of the basics.

Modern Correspondences

As well as the older correspondences, there are newer ones which may also be of interest. The time associated with each Few and Tree in Robert Graves' Tree Calendar is listed in case that is something you wish to add to your practice. Some of the Deity correspondences for each Few are older and come from older mythology such as Bran's link to the Alder Tree, others are newer and come from more recent folklore, Wicca, the Druid revival, and the like. The element, planet, crystal and other animal correspondences are all modern. Although they do fit rather well with the energies and lore of the relevant tree, which is why they are included, they do not have any historical basis and it's important for me to be honest about that with you.

Source Based Correspondences

Some of these correspondences are from older sources. The tree type within the eighth-century CE Brehon laws allows you to see how the ancient Celts viewed and how much reverence they attached to each tree. From *The Ogham Tract* I have included some of the Fews associations from some of the other, more relevant, Oghams. These are the Bird Ogham, the Colour Ogham and the People Ogham. The People Ogham can be useful to ascertain other players in the circumstances or can represent an aspect, or aspects, of yourself or others. The Bird Ogham and Colour Ogham can give you further insight because like the trees, birds and colours have many metaphysical, magical and mythological meanings that you can research as you develop your Ogham practice. Quite why each bird and colour is associated with each Few, as with the trees, could be because of some great esoteric and mystical meaning, but it could simply be practicality, or perhaps a mix of both.

Here is an example: Duir is *Duir* ('Oak'), *Dubh* ('Black') in the Colour Ogham, *Droen* ('Wren') in the Bird Ogham and *Dabach* ('Cask') in the Agricultural Ogham. While on the surface these seem to be connected simply because they all start with the letter 'D' that the Few Duir represents, once we start looking deeper into this, we can see that these things are connected, which is synchronicity and our brain's pattern recognition skills at work. Oak was and still is favoured for making casks for alcoholic beverages because its porous nature allows the contents to breathe and the Oak imparts its own qualities into the contents – European Oak adds a spiciness while American Oak is said to add a sweetness. The Wren is the King of Birds as the Oak is the King of Trees and the Wren is closely associated with the Oak tree in legend and lore. It was even nicknamed the Druid bird and we know that the Druids take their name from the Oak. So, it does seem that whoever composed these Oghams did carefully and deliberately consider which of all the many birds, colours, etc. that begin with that letter to use for that particular Ogham and relate it back to the tree that the Few represents.

The Word Oghams & Other Sources

As these are so fundamental to our understanding of the meaning ascribed to each of the Fews, and how each Few and associated tree was perceived by our ancestors, I have added these where possible. Some are quite obviously about the relevant tree, while others are cryptic. I hope they inspire you and add something to your understanding of the Ogham.

The General Explanation

This section begins with a little about the tree itself, where it likes to grow, how tall or small it is, and any interesting information about its leaves, flowers, fruit and nuts. This is to give you an overview and help you to identify them. Then we move on to what the tree represents, any folklore, myths or stories associated with it, and what it has come to mean in divination. It is not exhaustive and there is a lot more information out there if you want to delve deeper into their meaning and mysteries. I would strongly encourage you to add to this section in your own journal of Book of Shadows what each tree means to you personally and what it means within the culture that you were born into or live in.

Chapter 7

The Beith Aicme

Beith – Birch

Letter: B
Original Meaning: Birch, Gum or Resin
Keywords: Beginnings, Birth, Purification, Changes, Initiation
Tree Type in Brehon Laws: Commoner
Celtic Tree Calendar: Dec 24th – Jan 20th
Element: Air / Water
Deity: Arianrhod
Bird Ogham: Pheasant
Colour Ogham: White
People Ogham: One Man
Crystal: Clear or Milky Quartz
Planet: Venus

Word Oghams
Cuchulainn: *'Browed beauty, worthy of pursuit.'*
Oenghus: *'Most silvery of the skin.'*
Morann Mac Main: *'Faded trunk and fair hair.'*

General Explanation
The Birch is an elegant and very colourful tree whose beauty is

everchanging with the seasons. The Birch may appear delicate, fragile even, yet it is a very hardy and hardwood tree. It thrives in the temperate and even boreal climate of the Northern Hemisphere and can grow in some very unusual places. Here the Birch teaches us to be hardy, flexible and adaptable. We too can survive and thrive anywhere with courage, determination and dignity. Birch inspires us to deal gracefully with whatever comes our way.

The Birch is in the same family of deciduous trees as the Alder and Hazel. For a tree the Birch is actually quite short-lived: its lifespan is around fifty to seventy years which is on a par with that of a human, and they reach their various life stages at around the same time as we do. Perhaps this is in part why we humans have such a great affinity for the Birch.

The Birch is a pioneer tree. As the ice retreated at the end of the last ice age, Birch was one of the first trees to colonise the land; it still is one of the first trees to grow after land has been cleared. As its leaves and twigs fall and then decompose, it actually helps fertilise the ground for any plants and trees that follow on after it.

Beith derives from an ancient word for 'gum' or 'resin'. The Birch produces a sweet-tasting sap that can be drunk. It has long been considered an important source of nutrients and rather like the finest of wines. The Birch can also be used to make a tar which serves as a waterproofing agent. This could explain why Beith later became the Birch.

The Birch tree contains the life-giving power of the Earth Goddess and the Goddess of Spring. Birch is often considered a feminine tree and her traditional names include 'Lady of the Woods' and 'Browed Beauty' for the way her canopy hangs. Traditionally the Birch is a tree of the Goddess. In *The Golden Bough*, Sir James Frazer recorded events in which trunks of Birch were literally dressed up as a woman or goddess.[15] In the tales of Scotland and Ireland, Brighid, the Goddess of Healing, has a rod of Birch, which she uses to bring life back to the earth at Imbolc in early Spring.[16] This is symbolic of the fact that the Birch is one of the very first trees to leaf in Spring. Perhaps this is why the Birch is also the first tree of the Irish Ogham and the first Ogham was said to have been carved into Birch? Birch bark was long used as a medium for writing on before the use of paper, especially in India and Russia.

As the first of the Fews of the Ogham, Birch represents inception and new beginnings of all kinds. In Wales the Birch was often used for the Maypole which symbolised the fertility of the land at Beltane.[17] There is an old bit of Highland folklore that states if any animal is barren, its fertility can be restored by touching it with a wand or stick of Birch. It is a great tree to work with for anything to do with fertility, pregnancy and of giving birth, in terms of giving birth to babies and to giving birth to new ideas, or to assist you with turning over a new leaf and essentially birth a whole new you. Birch teaches us to embrace the new, to seize new opportunities and to continue to grow spiritually.

Birch is the tree of Initiation and of the first degree in High Wicca and of the Bard – the first grade – in Druidry. In *The Celtic Tree Calendar*, Birch governs the period from December 24th to January 20th and therefore, is seen to help sweep away the old year and usher in all the new opportunities of year ahead. Rods of Birch were used to literally drive out the spirits and energies of the old year. Both the Celts and Scandinavians used, and indeed still use, Birch in purification rituals to get rid of the old, negative, stagnant energies and welcome in the new. Finns still use bundles of Birch against the skin to encourage circulation during saunas, which is a traditional cleansing ritual in its own right. Birch was used to make the traditional witch's besom: its twigs are bound to the handle to form the bristles that sweep away the negativity and the dust bunnies.

When Birch appears in a reading, it is suggesting that this

is a time for a thorough Spring clean. This could be practical, spiritual or emotional. After all many of us hold on to our emotions just as soft furnishings hold dust. Birch assists in the cleansing release of old ways, bad habits, negative beliefs and negative energies. Shedding these will help you to make the most of the future.

If you are seeking answers, the Birch advises you to go back to the beginning. Go back to basics and hit the books or online search engines. Start over from scratch for you will find a new sense of direction and see things from a new perspective.

Traditionally a symbol of young love, love tokens, such as the Welsh lovespoons, were often carved form Birch. Birch suggests new love, or the rekindling of love in an existing relationship. It reminds us of the need to go back sometimes and look at why we first fell in love with someone and to re-create or re-invigorate that initial spark and attraction. It may also indicate a new activity or opportunity that you will love.

The Silver Birch was also thought to have been a portal to the Otherworld, as in Celtic Myth people or animals that were linked to the Otherworld often have a pale appearance. Throughout Siberia the Birch is their World Tree and served as a door or portal between the various worlds.[18] On moonlight nights the silvery-white bark of the Silver Birch does indeed appear to have a very ghostly or Otherworldly shine. This could well be why the Birch is held sacred to the many Moon Deities of the World. To the ancient Welsh the Birch was the Tree of Arianrhod – their Goddess of the Moon, Fate and Reincarnation, and a tree of the cycle of life, also known as the cycle of birth, death and reincarnation.

When Birch appears, it may be indicating that you need to undertake a spiritual journey or to re-evaluate where you are and where you are going on your spiritual path. Birch can help you to connect more deeply to all things spiritual, to the spirits, the ancestors and the Divine. It may also be portending a physical journey, a new job in a new location, a house move, a new relationship or a new addition to the family.

Birch urges us to be courageous and determined, and make the most of the cards we are dealt in life. Birch in a reading symbolises change, new opportunities and lots of wonderful blessings coming your way. It indicates that a previous phase is drawing to an end, while a new phase is opening up ahead of you. The lesson of the Birch is to learn to accept that change is inevitable; changes bring potential and new goals to be achieved. There is the opportunity of a fresh start, so seize it and make the most of it.

Beith Reversed

A time of stagnation or lack of movement. Things are not going ahead as planned. What started out promising appears no longer to be so. It suggests that you are stuck in a rut, now is a time to let go of the past and to move on. Change and the new are nothing to fear. Perhaps you feel as if you are going nowhere or simply going around in circles. Do you feel stuck in any way? What can you do to get things going again? Beith reversed can indicate that you need to make some serious and urgent changes in your life.

Luis – Rowan

Letter: L
Original Meaning: Flame or Herb

Keywords: Protection, Inspiration, Magic, Psychic Ability, Creativity
Tree Type in Brehon Laws: Commoner
Celtic Tree Calendar: Jan 21st – Feb 17th (includes Imbolc)
Element: Earth
Deity: Brighid, Ceridwen, Taranis
Bird Ogham: Duck
Other Animal: Dragon
Colour Ogham: Grey
People Ogham: Two Men
Other Colours: Green and Red
Crystal: Bluestone
Planet: Sun and the Stars

Word Oghams

Cuchulainn: *'Strength of cattle.'*
Oenghus: *'Friend of cattle.'*
Morann Mac Main: *'Delight of eye, the flame.'*

General Explanation

Although Luis originally meant 'flame' or 'herb', both terms can be equally applied to this very fiery tree of great healing and so perhaps this is why this Few was assigned the Rowan as its tree.

The Rowan is quite a small deciduous tree, usually growing between ten and twenty metres tall. Their leaves are pinnate and arranged alternatively, as is also seen with the Ash tree, hence its byname of Mountain Ash. The Rowan is not related to the Ash though, and is in fact one of the Rose family. With its vibrant red berries, pale white flowers and rich brown trunk, like other members of its family the Rowan is an extremely beautiful tree and has long been associated with beauty, love and creativity. When Celtic poets were waxing lyrical about a person's beauty, they would often compare the person to the Rowan as in the song *Marie's Wedding*:

'Red her cheeks as rowans are,
bright her eyes as any Star,
fairest of them all by far,
is our darling Marie.'

Even J.R.R. Tolkien embraced this tradition in his book *The Two Towers* where Quickbeam says of the Rowans, 'people of the Rose ... are so beautiful to me.'[19]

There is a theory that the beautiful and varied colours of the Rowan inspired the colours of the Clan Tartans in Scotland.[20] Certainly, the Rowan has been inspiring creativity in all its forms for a very long time. Traditionally spindles and spinning wheels were created from Rowan wood and so it became a tree of all kinds of crafts, witchy and otherwise. When Rowan appears in a reading it may be urging you to get creative, perhaps in terms of getting creative to solve a problem or to unleash your creative soul and create for the pleasure of it. Write, sing, dance, get out your hobby craft bit and bobs and make something. Enjoy the experience and allow it to uplift your soul.

In Celtic lore inspiration is a Divine gift or magical potion. The Celts considered the Rowan to be the *'Tree of Bards'* that bestowed on them the gift of inspiration. The magical brew in the cauldron of Ceridwen was a potion for inspiration or *awen,* and in Irish and Scottish lore Brighid was the Patron of the Arts and bestower of creative inspiration. The Celts of old described inspiration as *'A Fire in the Head'*[21] and anyone who has ever felt true and deep inspiration can empathise with that description.

This Divine inspiration was closely connected to Divine insight and magic. The Rowan is a tree of divination, insight and foreknowledge. The name Rowan may derive from an old Norse word for 'red', but it may also derive from *Rune,* an old word meaning 'secret' or 'magic'.[22] Rowan was one of the trees often used for carving the Norse Runes upon which were used for divination. Today it is still a very popular wood for magical tools and divination sets. Rowan allows us access to both ancient knowledge and the mystery of what is yet to come.

The Rowan is sacred to the Goddess in all her forms and is marked as a tree of the Goddess and of magic and protection. Its white flowers have five petals and thus resemble the pentagram – an ancient magical symbol of protection. Another pentagram can also be found when its red berries are cut in half.

Rowan is a tree of magic and was sacred to the Druids. When the Rowan is cast it portends that you find yourself about to enter a very magical and blessed time. Rowan inspires us to embrace the magic, to get creative with our own magical practice and to really be inspired by the magic that is all around us.

Several magical and mythical animals are associated with the Rowan such as the dragon, who represents the natural magical energies of the earth and the paths that such energy takes through the land. Rowan helps you to connect to the energies of the earth and the mysteries of nature. It is no coincidence that many Rowans are found near old stone circles or sites where dragons were said to have lived. Here the Rowan may be calling on you to connect more deeply with the land where you live in your magical and spiritual practice or to come back down to earth if you have been away with the fairies.

Rowan in a reading indicates potential danger and offers you protection. When Rowan is cast it reminds you of the need for protection, to take steps to protect yourself, your love ones and your home. Rowan speaks to us of both magical and practical steps to defend ourselves, such as creating protective charms or changing our passwords for online banking on a regular basis. There is much we can do to help ourselves and to help others.

Rowan tells you confidently to believe in yourself and reminds you that you that have within you the means and ability to deal with those potential dangers effectively, and that as with everything in life, you can and will learn from the experience and grow as a person. Adversity can be used create opportunities and generate great wisdom.

All parts of the Rowan are considered to offer protection, especially from malevolent magic or ill wishes. Berries are dried and threaded together to form charms and protective bracelets. Twigs of Rowan wood were tied together with red thread and placed over the doors of homes and barns to protect the people and animals who lived within. In the past cattle were considered especially vulnerable to black magic or being stolen away or harmed by fairies, so Rowan twigs were often placed in barns or tied around the necks of cattle. This is why Rowan is called *'friend of cattle'* in some of *The Word Oghams*. As Rowan was sacred to many Thunder Gods such as Thor and Taranis, twigs of Rowan were also placed on ships to protect them from storms. In the Art Ogham Rowan is *luamnacht* or 'pilotage'.[23]

These days we do not necessarily attribute misfortune to black magic, but Rowan does remind us of the negative energies and intentions we face in life every day and suggests to us a way to positively and creatively deal with them. Rowan offers us a magical shield of protection to deflect that negative energy and any negative magic away from us. Such dangers may not always come at us from an external source, sometimes we can be our own worst enemies. Our insecurities, lack of self-esteem, own negative attitudes and behaviours can be as much of a danger to our wellbeing as anything else. Rowan calls on you gently to turn these negative aspects around, to learn to see yourself for the beautiful and creative soul that you are.

Rowan is also a tree of life and of healing. Various parts of the tree have been used as medicine and conversely as a poison, and so Rowan may be indicating a need for you to look to and tend to your own health. This could be your physical, mental or spiritual health, or combination of all three. The Rowan is known as the 'Quicken tree', as in the quickening of energies and life force or the rising of the sap. This is why in *The Celtic Tree Calendar* it represents early Spring, from Jan 21st – Feb 17th, when life and nature is really starting to get going and get growing. Here it can represent a time of increased energy or activity, or be encouraging you to become more energetic and actively involved in what is currently going on in your life.

Luis Reversed

In this form Rowan shows that your defences are down and that you are wide open to attack from all fronts. Now is the time to build up your defences and to avoid patterns of destructive behaviour that are harming you and others around you. May indicate that a storm is coming and will shake things up. You may be feeling decidedly uninspired, so find ways to re-engage your creative spirit. Here the Rowan advises you to go inwards and connect to your own innate magic and to seek guidance from your deity or guides. Remember that magic is all around you and that you too are magical.

Fearn – Alder

Letter: F
Original Meaning: Alder
Keywords: Guidance, Shield, Confidence, Challenges
Tree Type in Brehon Laws: Commoner
Celtic Tree Calendar: Mar 18th – Apr 14th
Element: Water / Fire
Deity: Bran the Blessed
Bird Ogham: Hawk

Other Animal: Fox
Colour Ogham: Red
Other Colour: Purple
People Ogham: Three Men
Crystal: Amethyst
Planet: Mars

Word Oghams

Cuchulainn: *'Protection of the heart – a shield.'*
Oenghus: *'Guarding of milk, vessel containing milk.'*
Morann Mac Main: *'Shield of warrior-bands, alder is the material the shield was made from.'*

General Explanation

The Alder can be found, often in groups, growing in damp areas or along the banks of rivers and streams, for it – like the Willow – loves water. The Alder is in the same family of deciduous trees as Birch and Hazel. The Alder is the only broadleaved tree to have cones, through which it spreads its seeds. These cones appear quite delicate but in fact have hidden strengths, just like the Alder itself.

As Rowan is a magical and spiritual shield, the Alder is a physical shield that offers you protection. This refers to a very active defence and possibly even an offensive protection. The ancient Celts used Alder to make many of their shields.[24] It is the tree of the wise and compassionate warrior who fights for what he believes in and to protect those who cannot protect themselves. These warriors know to temper their great strength and power with kindness and generosity. They are like those ancient Knights of the Round Table who sought to undertake quests and do great deeds rather than simply fighting for the sake of it. Those knights formed a special fellowship and worked together to right wrongs and protect the people. Alder knows better than to go it alone; it knows that sometimes we need help from others and that the whole can be greater than the sum of its parts. A one-person crusade is rarely successful and so Alder calls upon you to engage with others, to essentially find and join your own fellowship and to offer them assistance and to ask for assistance when needed.

When Alder is cut, it appears to bleed, just as we do. Its bark is also used to make a very strong red dye. This is another reason it is the tree of the warrior who must sacrifice his own blood and shed that of his enemies. Alder is associated with the idea of lifeblood, that blood is quite literally the stuff of life and has magical powers.

The Alder in a reading speaks of challenges and battles ahead that you, like the warriors of old, need to face with courage, confidence and determination. It can also mean that you need to challenge the status quo in order to improve things for yourself or for others, say fighting for your rights or fighting to save the planet. It can also indicate that you need to challenge yourself to do more or to do better. You need to know whether to take up the sword or the shield for each particular battle or challenge that you face and that takes great wisdom and experience. Yet it can conversely indicate that you need to make peace, that this particular battle cannot be won with things as they currently are. Alder teaches you to wisely choose your battles and once chosen, to give it your all. Alder assures you that whatever battles you must face in life, they will make you stronger and hone your skills. You can work with Alder to increase your self-confidence, your personal strength and your willpower.

If you have achieved or are about to achieve victory or success, Alder reminds you to share the benefits of the success and the credit with others. It encourages team work and finding like-minded people to encourage and support you and with whom you can share your strength and skills.

As it is associated with the fox, Alder reminds you that battles are not always won with brute force, sometimes they need cunning, shrewdness, quick thinking, determination and above all patience. It encourages you to think of challenges as a problem to be solved, rather than to necessarily be attacked head on.

The Alder is associated with both fire, for its warrior aspect, and with water for it is close to water that the Alder likes to grow. Alder is famous for decaying very slowly when submerged in water – that which should destroy it only makes it stronger. So, Alder was used to build the crannogs or lake dwellings in Scotland,[25] to make causeways across marshes by the Romans and for the pilings that still form the foundations of the city of Venice.[26] Alder was also used to make containers for milk and was thought to help protect the milk from fairies who might otherwise steal it.

Alder is a sacred and protective spirit tree of Britain and in particular was sacred to the Welsh Giant God and Warrior King Bran the Blessed. Long before King Arthur was born, Bran was the Guardian of Britain. The legend tells us that Matholwch, King of the Irish asked Bran for his sister, Branwen's, hand in marriage, and the two were wed. However, things went very wrong from the start and Branwen was badly mistreated. Soon enough the armies of Matholwch and Bran were at war. All but a few of them were killed and Bran was mortally wounded. Bran told his men to cut off his head and bury it under the White Hill in London, where from that day forth he promised look out towards Europe and protect Britain from invasion.[27] That White Hill, according to legend, is where the Tower of London now stands. As you know, Britain has since been invaded quite a few times, and according to the story this is because many years after Bran's sacrifice, King Arthur came along and decided that he was more than capable of defending Britain so he dug up Bran's head, against the advice of those who knew the legend. As a result, Bran's protection was undone and the Saxons promptly invaded. Here Alder serves to warn us not to get overconfident or we will bring disaster upon ourselves and to pay attention when we are given sage and sound advice.

Before Bran's head was taken to London, for many years it spoke to and entertained his head which continued to speak, even though it had been severed from his body. This alludes to the fact that the Celts were obsessed with the head, they viewed it as the seat of wisdom, power and the soul. Severed heads like Bran's were considered to be oracles – to be able to offer deep wisdom, to reveal secrets or to predict the future – as Bran did when he claimed that his head would protect Britain. When Alder appears in a reading it is advising you to use your head. To think, to plan, to consult others and listen to their advice. Alder represents your inner voice, your thoughts your intuition and tells you to pay due attention to it. It may also be advising you to seek advice and guidance from your spirit guides and ancestors or to perform divination to help you to explore your thoughts on a particular matter. When Alder appears in a divination spread it is a fortuitous sign and shows that the advice contained in the reading is particularly valuable and apt for you at this time.

Alder Reversed

Alder reversed suggests that you are not listening to some very important advice, be it from your inner guidance or another person. It can also indicate that the advice you are getting is either plain bad or just not suitable for your circumstances. Now is a time to listen to the inner voice and to only listen to those that you trust. You may be feeling bogged down and unable to progress. Take some time to think and plan before trying to move things forward. Avoid conflict with others and stay out of things that do not concern you. Bide your time and wait for the right moment to make your move.

Saille – Willow

Letter: S
Original Meaning: Willow
Keywords: Intuition, Divination, Dreams, Emotions, Healing
Tree Type in Brehon Laws: Commoner
Celtic Tree Calendar: Apr 15th – May 12th
Element: Water
Deity: Ceridwen, Arianrhod, Adsagsona
Bird Ogham: Hawk
Other Animal: Cat
Colour Ogham: Fine-Coloured
Other Colour: Silver
People Ogham: Four Men
Crystal: Moonstone
Planet: Moon

Word Oghams
Cuchulainn: *'I sail, beginning of loss, willow.'*
Oenghus: *'Activity of bees, for its bloom and for its catkin.'*
Morann Mac Main: *'Hue of the lifeless.'*

General Explanation
The Willow is a graceful, water-loving tree that – like the Alder – can be found along the banks of waterways and in other wet zones. The leaves are typically elongated and quite varied in the tones of green as some are yellow green, others are a blue-green

and others quite a silver green. Willows are one of the first trees to leaf in Spring and one of the last to lose their leaves come Autumn. Technically Willows are a family of trees rather than one specific tree.

With its link to water the Willow is a tree of healing, especially emotional and spiritual healing. If Willow has appeared, it is calling upon you to pay attention to your well-being. Willow advises you to speak to your health professional about any health concerns that you may have, to make sure you get your regular check-ups, to review and take any medications you need, and to look at what you do to heal and take care of yourself. It can be advising you to take a long, healing soak in the bath, to take some time off work to rest or do whatever you need to do to feel healed and rested.

In particular Willow asks you to take good care of your emotional health. Willow reminds us of the power and depth of our own emotions. When Willow turns up it can be pointing out to you that you are ignoring your own emotions at your peril. It advises us against bottling them up and gently teaches us how to let them go. As the Weeping Willow, Willow reminds us that it is OK to cry, to weep and let our emotions out, especially in the form of tears. Willow encourages us to be emotionally honest with ourselves and to work with our emotions and how we feel about things in order to truly understand ourselves.

Various parts of the Willow are famed for their medicinal properties. In ancient Egypt the leaves were used to treat fevers and various aches and pains.[28] In Britain Willow bark was used for treating and counteracting ailments that were associated with damp, such as the ague (which probably refers to malaria) and rheumatic diseases such as arthritis.[29] One old name for the Willow is 'Witch's Aspirin'.[30] The bark is famous for containing salicin, which metabolises into salicyclic acid once consumed, and was the inspiration for the creation of Aspirin and nonsteroidal anti-inflammatory drugs or NSAIDs which are used to treat a wide variety of ailments and thin the blood. Essentially it is the Willow that gave us what is now the most widely prescribed medicine in the world.[31]

As bees flock to the Willow for its nectar rich catkins in Spring, the Willow is associated with fertility. It also roots extremely easily from cuttings or even where branches have just fallen to the ground. In fact, some modern gardeners and herbalists use powdered Willow in place of hormone rooting powder to encourage other plants to take root when propagating. Willow is also fast growing so can indicate growth in a reading or the creation of something new as well as possible pregnancies and births. There was once an idea that if a Willow leaf fell onto a pregnant woman or her clothes if they were left out to dry, that her delivery would be smooth, so Willow suggests that plans and projects will go smoothly.

The Willow tree is known by many names: Osier, Sally, and Sallow, the last of which has is also the word to describe the unhealthy pallor of a sick person's skin. It is perhaps best known though as the Weeping Willow for the way its canopy hangs. Here we see the Willow associated with illness, grief and death and so in a reading it can portend illness, the need to grieve and heal after loss, a death or the end of something, as in the end of a project, finishing university or the end of a career as someone retires. To 'Wear the Willow' as in to wear a sprig on your clothes or hat was a sign that a person was grieving for a loved one or who were forsaken in love.[32] To the ancient Celts death was as tragic as it is to us, but they also believed that death was one of the stages in the natural cycle of life, death and rebirth. For centuries it was traditional to place Willow branches in coffins with the deceased or to plant a Willow on a grave for it was said: 'Plant a Willow, allow it to grow, to ease the passage of the soul at death'. Such Willows were thought to serve as a bridge between this world and the next and provide a means of communication with the dead. Here Willow may mean changes that at first seem very unpleasant, but that ultimately will help you grow, lead to positive changes and work out for the best.

The Willow is a tree of magic, especially lunar magic, dreams, the Otherworld, psychic powers, divination and witches. It was even known as the *'Tree of Enchantment'*.[33] Willow was used to bind the witches' besom together and many divinatory and magical tools were and still are crafted from Willow such as wands, Runes and Ogham Staves. This is because Willow opens us up spiritually to the worlds around us. Willow encourages you to hone your natural psychic skills and intuition and may indicate that your skills and emotions are awakening or developing. Yet Willow also advises us to remain firmly grounded in reality.

Due to its link with the Moon, the Willow was and is considered sacred to the Celtic Moon and Magic Deities such as the little known Adsagsona – A Celtic Goddess of Magic and the Underworld, *Arianrhod* – whose name means 'Silver Wheel' a likely reference to the spinning Stars of the firmament or the Full Moon and *Ceridwen* – whose name may mean something like 'White Crooked One' as in the crescent moon. When Willow appears, it may be reminding you to look to the Moon, to its phase and its magic and the energies prevalent at this time. It may also be asking you to pay attention to your dreams and visions or that now is a good time to start trying to bring your dreams into reality.

The Willow has been utilised in handicrafts for around ten thousand years, hence it being listed as *sairsi* or 'handicrafts' in the Art Ogham.[34] Baskets, fencing, furniture, houses, rope and coracles – a type of small round boat that was much beloved by the Celts, have traditionally been made with shoots from the Willow. So, Willow can represent a time of creative energy or a practical need to repair or rebuild something in your life.

If you want to get a clearer view of events, things or people, use your emotion and intuition rather than cold logic at this time. Willow encourages you to listen to your emotions, to decide how you really feel about the situation at hand before you make any decisions.

Willow is about going with the flow in life, but not to the point where you lose control over your life. You still need to be the captain of your own ship and heading it in the direction you want to go in.

Saille Reversed

When Willow is reversed it suggests that you are out of your depth and that you are getting carried away by events or emotions. Willow reversed is warning you that you have not been taking very good care of yourself, perhaps you have been too busy taking care of others or other things. Maybe you feel that everything is running away from you at the moment or you feel distracted or lost. Now is the time to try to get back control of your life. It may also be advising you to seek very practical solutions to your problems.

Nuinn – Ash

Letter: N
Original Meaning: Forked or Lofty
Keywords: Change, Order, Harmony, Balance
Tree Type in Brehon Laws: Chieftain
Celtic Tree Calendar: Feb 18th – Mar 17th
Element: Air

Deity: Manannan, Gwydion
Bird Ogham: Snipe
Other Animal: Adder
Colour Ogham: Clear
People Ogham: Five Men
Crystal: Turquoise
Planet: The Whole Universe

Word Oghams
Cuchulainn: *'Flight of beauty, of weaver's beam.'*
Oenghus: *'Flight of women, of weaver's beam.'*
Morann Mac Main: *'Checking of peace.'*

General Explanation
The Ash is known as the World Tree or Cosmic Axis, in part because of its great height. It is commonly believed that Yggdrasil, the World Tree of the Vikings was an Ash, though some say a Yew.[35] The World Tree connects all three realms: the Upperworld of the deities, the Middle World of Humans and the Underworld or Realm of the Dead. According to Iolo Morganwg, who, frankly, did make stuff up, the Celts also believed that existence came in the form of three realms through which we pass, in their case Abred – the realm of the living, Gwynfyd – the afterlife and Ceugant – which is infinity or the realm of the Spiritual and Divine.[36] Here Ash informs you how everything in the Universe is interconnected, that our actions have consequences and that our pasts have led us to our present circumstances. Ash reminds you of your Karma and to learn from your past. Ash allows you to predict the future, based on the past and present, and to see where things are going. If you do not like the direction things are taking, Ash offers you the chance to make suitable changes – externally or internally – to change your fate.

When Ash appears in a reading it can be calling on you to

evaluate your own connections to the worlds around you, your connection to your family and friends, your work colleagues, to nature and to the Divine. It is advising you to make more connections and to strengthen those that you already have. It emphasises the importance of connections and of feeling connected to the world. Humans are after all a social species.

Ash reminds you that you are an emotional, physical and spiritual being and calls on you to find balance within, for this tree symbolises balance and harmony. The leaves of the Ash grow opposite each other on the stem so seem to balance each other out. If you are asking about a situation, Ash indicates that it will be a harmonious one. It can also emphasise the need for teamwork and to get all of the team involved in order to achieve success.

Nuinn is thought to derive from a combination of words from the various Celtic languages that mean things like 'lofty' and 'heaven' for its great height and Universal connection and 'forked' for its branches. Its forked branches are what make the Ash so easy to spot, even in Winter as the branches seem to curve downwards and then rise again to the heavens. In ancient times the Celts waved these distinctive forked branches during battles to call a halt – permanent or temporary – to hostilities, hence it being referred to as *'the checking of peace'*.

Ash wood was also used to make spears, and the English word for Ash derives from a Germanic word for 'spear'. Spears are protective and offensive weapons that are ideal for keeping your enemy at a distance rather than allowing them to get too close and so here Ash can be advising you to keep your distance from your enemies as in those who may wish you harm in some way such as the office gossip or a work rival. Ash calls upon you to protect yourself and those you are closely connected to.

The Ash tree is also sacred to the Celtic Sea God – Manannan Mac Lir, who had magical spear made from the Ash, and the Ash tree was said to have originated in his kingdom, which could either refer to the sea or to the Isle of Man which is named for him. Also, from Celtic legends we learn that Gwydion – a magician and shapeshifter, had a wand made from Ash. Ash wands are particularly favoured by men, perhaps owing to the Norse myth that the first man, Askr, was created from the Ash tree,[37] and are often used for what was traditionally considered men's magic. There are many examples of wands made from Ash from the archaeological record, including one found on the Isle of Anglesey in Wales that is over two thousand years old. Ash is another tree, like the Birch, that was traditionally used to make the handle for the witches' besom.[38] As the Ash connects and is part of all three worlds or realms, there is the idea that wands, besoms and other magical tools made from Ash allow the magical practitioner to journey into and between all of the realms of existence. Its seeds are called 'keys', perhaps in reference to the fact that the Ash is essentially the key to accessing to entire Cosmos.

There is also the notion that as the Ash grows so high, it allows you to see things from a totally new and perhaps more spiritual perspective. When Ash appears, it asks you to look at things in a whole new way or is suggesting that you need to get a much clearer overview of what is going on in order the make the best decision.

The Ash tree is one of the last trees to leaf in Spring. In this Ash reminds us that it is perfectly OK to be a late bloomer, to be the last to hear or know something, or be late to the party – the Ash is still beautiful when it does finally get around to spreading its leaves. In a reading Ash can, therefore, indicate delays or things taking much longer than expected, but do not worry, for things will still turn out just fine.

Along with the Oak and Thorn, Ash is one of the Fairy Triad and where they grow fairies are found. As well as attracting fairies and butterflies the Ash seems to attract lightning, and yet at the same time is able to withstand storms so Ash may be letting you know that a storm is coming, but that you will be able to weather it.

Looms were often made from the Ash, hence the references in *The Word Oghams* to *'weaver's beams'* and Ash can be split and woven to make things like baskets. The wood of the Ash is tough and yet elastic. Ash teaches us to be strong and courageous like the spear wielding warrior, but also reminds us to be flexible and open to negotiation. Despite its strength, Ash wood rots in water so advises us that no matter how strong someone is, we all have our weaknesses as well as our strengths. There is strength in numbers though, so Ash calls upon us to work with others and to call upon the powers and the energies around us at this time.

One of the most important messages from the Ash is that we are a part of nature, part of creation and part of the great cycle of life, death and rebirth. Ash urges us to find inner peace and outer peace by finding balance within ourselves and a balance with others and the rest of the Cosmos. As a tree of universal truth, it calls upon us to be honest and to be our authentic selves.

Ash Reversed

In this form Ash indicates that you are not feeling in control of your life. You may be feeling lonely, separated or cut off from the world. Perhaps you find yourself stuck in a cycle of events or emotions from which you cannot escape. Ash indicates that current circumstances are ultimately of your own making and reminds you that you have the power and strength to change them for the better, especially if you seek help from others. Ash reversed may also be advising you to look at things up close and in great detail before you make any important decisions.

Chapter 8

The Huathe Aicme

Huathe – Hawthorn / Whitethorn

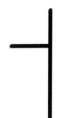

Letter: H
Original Meaning: Hawthorn or Fear
Keywords: Obstructions, Obstacles, Being Held Back, Healing
Tree Type in Brehon Laws: Commoner
Celtic Tree Calendar: May 13th – Jun 9th & May 1st / Beltane
Element: Air
Deity: Olwen, The Morrighan
Bird Ogham: Raven
Colour Ogham: Terrible-Coloured
Other Colours: Deep Blue and Purple
People Ogham: One Woman
Crystal: Lapis Lazuli
Planet: Saturn

Word Oghams & Other Sources
Cuchulainn: *'Difficult night, hawthorn.'*
Oenghus: *'Blanching of face due to fear.'*
Morann Mac Main: *'For a terror to any one is a pack of wolves.'*
Battle of the Trees: *'The hawthorn, surrounded by prickles, With pain at his hand.'*

General Explanation

The Hawthorn is a small and shrubby tree with smooth grey bark, distinctive lobed leaves, pale and richly scented white flowers and rich red fruits, known as haws. When the wood of this tree is burned, it burns with an intense and fierce heat, hence its association with fire and air. Its delicate flowers have five petals which form a pentagram shape and its fruits contain up to five stone-like pyrenes, so the Hawthorn is considered a tree of the Goddess and of protection.

The Hawthorn, as the name suggests, bears some very vicious thorns which can cause serious damage and great pain. Its thorns may invoke fear in some, hence *The Word Ogham's* references to difficulties, fear and wolves, and the fact that its very name derives from an old Irish word for fear, but this is perhaps a bit of a misunderstanding. Hawthorns were used in times past instead of fencing to keep certain things in and other things out. Its thorns are not aggressive, but defensive. The Hawthorn seeks only to protect itself and the others to whom it offers shelter, such as birds and bugs.

Hawthorn is believed to offer us protection from many different things, from thunder and lightning, evil witches, ghosts, bad fairies and even vampires. In a reading Hawthorn calls upon you to protect yourself from negative energies and entities and to set up a defensive barrier to keep you safe. This message is doubly important if it appears alongside Luis / Rowan. It calls on you to establish and assert your own boundaries in a safe and productive way.

With its sharp thorns and its connection to the raven in the Bird Ogham,[39] this Few has become linked with The Morrighan, the powerful and fearsome Goddess of War, Sovereignty and Protector of the Land who was said to transform herself into the shape of a crow or raven.

Hawthorn may indicate disempowerment, entanglement, getting stuck and being held back. Do not allow yourself to get tangled up in the issue at hand or the machinations of others. Hawthorn suggests obstructions, obstacles and people getting in your way and preventing you from making progress. We cannot fell this tree that we find blocking our path, for according to both ancient folklore and modern urban legends, to fell a Hawthorn brings disaster. Neither can you push on and hope for the best at this time because its spiky thorns will stop you. However, do not become downhearted by this lack of progression for Hawthorn here is offering you a blessing in disguise. It may well be that Hawthorn is stopping you from making a mistake, protecting you from something, or allowing something bad to completely pass you by. Be patient, step back and embrace this gift of some much-needed down time. If you think about it for much of nature Winter is down time and a chance to rest and recuperate before springing forth again. Make the most of this time to plan and think, to rest, research, seek out new opportunities, re-evaluate and take stock of what is going on in your life.

In Britain the Hawthorn is an integral part of our hedgerows which have literally become a lifeline for many species of flora and fauna. It is the spirit tree of the traditional solitary hedge witch, who studies the wisdom of plants and the natural world and weaves magic into their everyday life. Hawthorn may be advising you to take some time out, to spend some time alone or to seek magic in the mundane. Hawthorn calls on you to explore the magic of nature, its cycles and the magic deep withing yourself.

Hawthorn is the most fairy of all trees. According to Irish and Scottish folklore every single Hawthorn, no matter where it grows, is rumoured to be both a portal and a barrier to Fairyland, depending on whether or not the fairies seek fit to grant you access. It is one of the Fairy Triad along with the Oak and the Ash. The Hawthorn is sacred to many Fairy Queens and Goddesses. According to Welsh legend the beautiful Giantess Olwen was the daughter of Ysbaddaden – the Hawthorn Giant, and wherever she walked white flowers bloomed. In some versions these are white trefoils, and in some others, they are Hawthorn flowers.[40] Also, from Wales comes the story of Blodeuwedd ('flower face') who was created from nine sacred plants, including the Hawthorn, as a wife for Llew.[41]

The Hawthorn is intimately associated with the Celtic Festival of Beltane and with the month of May, because it is in May that the Hawthorn, also known as the May Tree,[42] flowers. In the Celtic Tree Calendar Hawthorn rules over the time of the Old Beltane Rites, the time when Beltane occurred under the old Julian Calendar. In some places the Maypole was traditionally made from a Hawthorn and it came to be seen as a tree of fertility. In a reading Hawthorn may refer to either Beltane or be portending a fertile time ahead. It indicates abundance, growth and things blossoming nicely.

As well as being a tree with a reputation for harm, the Hawthorn is also a tree of healing. Many Hawthorns are found near sacred sites, especially as rag or clooties trees, which are decorated trees that protect old holy and healing wells and springs. There is an extremely ancient tradition, still actively practiced today, where a biodegradable piece of cloth or rag is dipped into the water of the holy well, rubbed on whatever part of your body is causing your health problems and then tied to the branches of a rag tree. As the rag fades over time and eventually disintegrate, the ailment is also said to fade away.

In folk medicine Hawthorn has long been used for healing, especially for healing ailments of the heart,[43] whether physical or emotional. It is also frequently used in love spells and divination on matters of love. It is after all a relative of the Rose – the flower of love. Hawthorn indicates matters of the heart when it appears in a reading and tells you that you already know the answer in your heart. It can portent romance or be calling on you to be more romantic or loving in your relationship. Hawthorn calls on you to take good care of your heart health and to deal with any emotional blockages that are holding you back. Hawthorn encourages self-love, love for your friends and family, love for nature and love for life. Hawthorn can help you to heal a broken heart and heal from life's disappointments.

Hawthorn offers us difficult challenges, but through facing them and overcoming them, we grow, learn and thrive. It never really gives us more than it knows we can handle. Hawthorn is a pretty, yet tough little tree, more than capable of holding its own. It is able to grow in all sorts of places and deal with all the crazy weather that Mother Nature throws at it and still it creates its wonderful flowers, fruits and leaves which offer us nourishment and healing. The Hawthorn inspires us to love life and live it to the full even when life itself is getting us down. In the language of flowers, the Hawthorn represents hope.

Huathe Reversed

You have reached an impasse. Hawthorn is asking you to rethink your path ahead and suggesting that this may not be the way for you to go. You may be feeling lonely, unloved or heart-broken, so Hawthorn encourages you to reminisce about old times when you felt loved, adored or happy in your heart and to find ways to feel that again. Learn to love yourself and to like yourself, after all you are stuck with yourself. Life is full of bad times and good times and without one we cannot fully appreciate the other.

Duir – Oak

Letter: D
Original Meaning: Oak

Keywords: Protection, Strength, Nobility, Endurance
Tree Type in Brehon Laws: Chieftain
Celtic Tree Calendar: Jun 10th – Jul 17th (includes the Summer Solstice)
Element: Earth
Deity: Dagda, Taranis
Bird Ogham: Wren
Colour Ogham: Black
People Ogham: Two Women
Crystal: Diamond
Planet: Jupiter

Word Oghams & Other Sources
Cuchulainn: *'Kneeling work, bright and shining work.'*
Oenghus: *'Carpenter's work.'*
Morann Mac Main: *'Highest of bushes, with respect to its wood in the forest.'*
Battle of the Trees: *'A valiant doorkeeper.'*

General Explanation
In Summer and Autumn, the Oak is always easy to spot due to its lobed shaped leaves which are arranged in a spiral and its distinctive acorns. In Spring it produces both male and female flowers in the form of catkins. The Oak grows to great heights and a very great age. Marton Oak, perhaps the oldest in the UK, has a girth of over 14 metres and is thought to be over a thousand years old.[44] It is a deciduous tree and is most at home in woodland.

No other tree is more linked in the modern psyche to the Celts and the Druids than the Oak tree. The title of Druid is said to derive from the Oak tree and mean something akin to 'Oak-Wise' implying that the Druids know the secrets of this amazing tree.[45] Even today the Oak is the tree of the third grade of Druidry – that of the Druid. The Romans described how the Druids worshipped the Oak tree and performed their rites in groves of Oak. The Druids considered the Mistletoe to sacred above all else, especially when it grew upon the Oak, and they considered it a gift from the Gods.[46] In the Art Ogham of *The Ogham Tract*, this is the Few of the art of *Druidheacht*, which is translates as Druidry.[47]

The wren, which is linked to this Few in the Animal Ogham[48] was a sacred bird that symbolised wisdom and divinity to the Druids and was known as the 'King of Birds'.[49]

Throughout Europe Oak trees have been considered sacred to the Sky Gods, those of Thunder, Lightning and Agriculture, such as the Greek Zeus, the Celtic Taranis and the Norse Thor.[50] With its high statue and the wood's low electrical resistance the Oak is struck by lightning more than most other trees and such strikes were seen as a message from the Gods. Zeus, the King of the Greek Gods, was said to speak to his followers through the rustling of the leaves of a great and ancient oracular Oak tree located at Dodona, in the mountains of north-western Greece.[51] Here the Oak tree serves as a doorway between humans and the gods through which we can communicate. According to folklore to carry a piece of lightning struck Oak wood on your person afforded you the protection of the Sky Gods and would prevent you from being struck by lightning. Carrying acorns was said to bring luck, so Oak may represent you being blessed by a stroke of good luck!

The Oak is also a sacred tree to the Dagda, the King and Father figure of the Irish Gods who was the God of Magic, Wisdom, Agriculture and Strength and who had the power over Life and Death.[52] According to legend the Dagda had a magic staff made of Oak that could kill a person with one end and bring them back to life with the other. One of the Dagda's many names was *Dáire* ('fruitful') and derives from the Irish for the Oak tree.

Several Celtic Goddesses are also associated with the Oak tree. Although today Druantia – the Queen of the Druids according to Robert Graves and a Goddess of Trees, Wisdom and Creativity – is thought of more as a Goddess of the Pine, her name alludes to the fact that she may once have been a Goddess of the Oak. The Welsh Blodeuwedd who was created as a wife for Llew was crafted from the flowers of the Oak[53] and a little-known Welsh Deity by the name of Daron – again from the Oak tree – lends their name to the River Daron/Aberdaron.[54] The pan-Celtic Goddess and later Christian Saint, Brighid, was said to have set up her Pagan Temple and later Christian Church beneath an ancient Oak called Brighid's Oak, which led to the place being named the 'Church of the Oak' or Kildare as we know it today.[55]

Due to its close association with so many deities, Oak is telling you loud and clear that you need to connect to and listen to the divine, that the divine has a really important message for you at this time.

Merlin, the Magician, Druid and adviser to King Arthur, was associated with the Oak tree. His magic wand was created from an Oak tree to which he had a special affinity and beneath whose boughs he liked to practice his magic. The tree is now known as Merlin's Oak and, although the original is long gone, a replacement Oak tree still stands in the very same position on the corner of Oak Lane and Priory Street in Carmarthen, which in Welsh is *Caerfyrddin* or 'Merlin's Fort'[56]. Today Oak is a popular wood for magic wands, staffs and divination tools.

The connection between kingship and the Oak is buried deep in the British psyche and it is a symbol of the United Kingdom. The Oak is the 'King of the Woods'. King Arthur's Round Table as crafted from Oak,[57] King Charles II, hid in an Oak tree in Boscobel Wood to escape the Roundheads after the Battle of Worcester in 1651CE[58] and 'The Oak' or 'The Royal Oak' is one of the most common names for pubs. In the *Celtic Tree Calendar*, the Oak rules from June 10th to July 17th; its energies are thought to be especially prominent at Midsummer when the Oak King, who rules over the lighter half of the year, fights the Holly King, who rules over the darker half of the year.

The Oak in a reading is calling on you to valiantly defend

yourself and others. It advises you to seek protection and assistance from the divine, from kingly or fatherly figures in your life that you can trust. Oak advises you to take the high road, to handle the situation with nobility and dignity. It is calling on you to do what you think is best for everyone – for the entire kingdom – rather than just doing what is best for you.

The Oak tree is often seen as its own kingdom because it provides for so many creatures. The Oak gives generously of itself, like a kindly king who truly cares for as well as protects his great kingdom. It even provides two sets of leaves in a year because it knows how much the bugs love to munch on them. Its wood provides a great deal of heat and burns slowly, its acorns were once a food source, its wood was used for making ships, houses and furniture and is much beloved by carpenters even today for its may qualities and its various parts were all considered valuable healing remedies. As a generous provider, Oak calls on you to give freely of yourself and to give with an open and generous heart.

It is said that the roots of the Oak go as far into the ground as its branches go into the air, so like the Ash it is perceived to be connected to all the worlds and realms of existence. The name *Duir* derives from an ancient term meaning 'Door'. The Oak is a door through which we can journey both in a physical sense because Oak opens up the path ahead for us and spiritually for it provides us access to the divine and the spiritual. After the obstacles of Huathe / Hawthorn, the Oak as Duir clears to way for you and presents you with an open doorway through which you can now progress. Doors are literally opening up for you, all you need to do is choose which one to go through. This also serves as the door to your own inner spirituality, to your inner strength and your inner self.

As the tree is set firmly in the ground, because its wood is so tough and because it lives for a very long time, the Oak symbolises strength and endurance. Oak may be asking you to endure the situation, but assures you that you do have the inner strength and willpower to be able to do so, even if you have to dig down deep. You can and will overcome adversity and you will grow to be mighty.

When Oak appears it is informing you that the situation is stabilising and that as long as you remain honest with yourself and others, harmony will be restored. Here too the Oak asks that you remain loyal and faithful in your dealings with others, in your relationship, with your colleagues and with yourself. Know that with the Oak at your side, you are on the right path and will be victorious.

Duir Reversed

Here Oak calls on you to examine your own motives and actions. It suggests that you may not be acting in the best interests of yourself and others. May indicate that you are abusing your authority, becoming too greedy or showing too much weakness to others who may soon take advantage. It calls on you to act more honourably. Can also suggest that you are ignoring important messages from the divine or not listening to advice.

Tinne – Holly

Letter: T
Original Meaning: Iron Bar or Ingot
Keywords: Patience, Testing, Defence, Sacrifice, Soul-Searching
Tree Type in Brehon Laws: Chieftain

Celtic Tree Calendar: Jul 18th – Aug 4th
Element: Earth and Fire
Deity: Llew / Lugh
Bird Ogham: Starling
Other Animal: War-Horse
Colour Ogham: Dark Grey
Other Colour: Blood Red
People Ogham: Three Women
Crystal: Ruby, Bloodstone
Planet: Mars / Saturn

Word Oghams & Other Sources

Cuchulainn: *'Third of weapons, iron bar forged in fire.'*
Oenghus: *'Fires of coal, that is holly.'*
Morann Mac Main: *'One of three parts of a wheel.'*
Battle of the Trees: *'Holly, it was tinted with green, He was the hero.'*

General Explanation

The Holly is easily spotted, especially in winter, with its deep green spiny leaves, its greenish-white flowers and rich red berries. Holly trees tend to be either male or female, with only the female producing berries. The Holly can be quite shrubby or it can form quite an elegant tree shape. Unlike most other trees the Holly grows very slowly and so always calls on us to be patient when it shows up in a reading.

To the Celts the Holly and the Oak were similar and yet different, rather like two sides of the same coin. While the Oak is a kindly and generous king always looking to assist and protect others from harm, the Holly is a thoughtful king who looks first to govern his internal self and to fighting internal battles in order to become a stronger, wiser and a better king.

According to folklore the Holly is most powerful during the dark of the year, a time when the Holly King is said to reign while the Oak is most powerful during the lighter half of the year when the Oak King rules. There are two versions of how the year is divided in this way. Some say that the darker half of the year runs between the Midsummer Solstice and Midwinter Solstice when the days are shortening and the lighter half runs from Midsummer to when the days are lengthening. Others divide the year so that the dark half runs from the Autumn Equinox to the Spring Equinox and the lighter half runs from the Spring Equinox to the Autumn Equinox.

According to the first version, the Oak King is born at the time of the Midwinter Solstice. As the days lengthen the Oak King grows and becomes more powerful until he is killed by the Holly King at the Midsummer Solstice. As the length of the day begins to wane, the Holly King grows in strength until he is sacrificed at the Midwinter Solstice, when we symbolically cut down Holly and use it to decorate our homes. Ultimately this story is all about the balance of light and dark, of the internal and external, of waxing energies and waning energies, and the cycle of life, death and rebirth. The Holly, therefore, symbolises balance and harmony. In a reading Holly portends a time of balance, with things progressing slowly but surely in the right direction, just like the turning of the seasons. In a reading this Few can refer to Midwinter or to its month in *The Celtic Tree Calendar* when the power of the Holly is starting to increase now that Midsummer is behind us and the days are getting shorter.

Holly may be calling upon you to make a sacrifice, to give something up in order to help others or to grow as a person. Here Holly particularly calls upon us to give up bad habits, negative emotions, and to cut those people out of our lives who are causing us harm in any way. As nature abhors a vacuum, Holly encourages us to bring strength, self-love and compassion into the space that we have just cleared in our heart, mind and soul.

The Holly King thrives on darkness and indeed the Holly will grow just as well in the shade as the sun, if not better. This is because the Holly King makes the most of the darkness to do some serious soul-searching and to get to know his true inner self. He knows that he is a deep and spiritual being and seeks to truly know and master himself. Holly wishes you to become your own master and to be in control of your own destiny. Holly can assist you in fighting your own inner demons, calming inner turmoil, and letting go of any negative feelings, such as jealousy or hatred. Holly understands the deep pain that we all hold inside and encourages us to turn it into something positive and beneficial rather than letting it fester and eat away at us. When Holly is cast it advises you to go within to seek your answers and sort things out.

Like the Ash, the Holly is closely associated with weapons. Spear shafts were sometimes made of Holly as were chariots. The Irish Hero, Nadcranntail, crafted nine such spears from Holly boughs.[59] Both spears and chariots require direction in order to be effective, a spear has to be thrown in the right direction for it to hit its mark and a chariot and its war-horses must be steered. Here Holly indicates that either you are going in the right direction or that you need to get back on track to get to where you wish to go in life. Holly can also provide spiritual direction when you are feeling a little lost and wondering if the path you are on is the right one for you.

Originally the Few of Holly may have referred to the charcoal made from the Holly, which was considered especially fine, or to the iron ingots that were used to forge weapons. Holly is ruled by the element of fire and the word *Tinne* is related etymologically to the word 'tinder'. Here we see the Holly is rather like the blacksmith of old – a magician of a kind who transforms things from one state of being to another, so Holly speaks to us of inner and spiritual transformation as we are forged by the challenges that life gives us. The Sword in the Stone is an allegorical tale based on how the smith transforms rock, or rather iron ore, into a finely crafted sword. It is a process of slow progress that requires patience and hard work. We too are works in progress and one day we too will pull the sword from the stone and become king, even if only in the sense of being master of our own unique self.

Even in the darkest of times, Holly as an evergreen offers us inspiration and hope. The always green leaves serve as a powerful reminder that the good days will return and life will once again return. Its bright berries bring cheer the soul, especially as they bring the birds who like to eat them and then sing their hearts out as if thanking the Holly for its abundance at a time when hardly any other food is available for them. Holly encourages us to seek out the good, to seek out happiness even in the darkness or sadness.

Holly is associated with the Celtic God Lugh or Llew who was the Shining God of Smithing, Metallurgy, Kingship and Law. Lugh was said to have possessed an unstoppable fiery spear whose shaft was made of Holly (though some say Yew) and whose five points had been forged in a fire fuelled by Holly charcoal.[60] *Lughnasadh,* which occurs on August 1st, right during the time the Holly rules in *The Celtic Tree Calendar* and folklore, is 'The Festival of Lugh'.

The Holly is associated with the idea of justice and so can indicate legal matters or the need to obtain justice. It warns you to stay within the law and not to seek vengeance. The Holly asks us to be just and fair in our dealings with others. By keeping a strong sense of justice, you will be able to overcome any obstacles and achieve a fair and well-deserved victory. Like the Holly itself, be steadfast, strong and courageous as you face the challenges that life has dealt you. Keep your spirit up, even during the hardships. Maintain your sense of identity and your precious inner balance.

Tinne Reversed

Holly reversed suggests that you are currently feeling like a victim of circumstance. Are you a victim of yourself or your own actions? Perhaps you feel that you have lost your inner strength or are feeling vulnerable? When reversed Holly suggests now is not the time to take action, rather now is the time to retreat in order to rebuild your inner defences and inner strength. There is no shame in a tactical retreat, rather it is a wise move. If you are feeling lost or lacking direction, Holly can help point you in the right direction, but it is down to you to take those first steps to get you back on track. One step at a time, even if it is slow and unsteady, is enough to get you going again.

Coll – Hazel

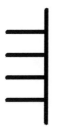

Letter: C
Original Meaning: Hazel
Keywords: Wisdom, Divination, Inspiration, Intuition
Tree Type in Brehon Laws: Chieftain
Celtic Tree Calendar: Aug 5th – Sep 1st
Element: Air / Water
Deity: Oenghus, Canola, Manannan and Brigid.
Animal: Salmon
Colour Ogham: Brown / Orange
People Ogham: Four Women
Crystal: Topaz
Planet: Mercury
Word Oghams & Other Sources
Cuchulainn: *'Sweetest of woods, a nut.'*

Oenghus: *'Friend of nutshells.'*
Morann Mac Main: *'Fairest of trees, owing to its beauty in woods.'*
Battle of the Trees: *'Hazel-trees, it was judged, that ample was thy mental exertion.'*

General Explanation

The Hazel is a rather lovely shrubby tree that can often be found growing in deciduous woodlands, hedgerows, in copses and in particular near streams and ponds, because – like the Willow – it does love water. Their catkins, which resemble golden tassels, appear in Spring before the leaves and really do make the tree stand out amongst the others. Some despise these catkins though for the pollen they release can be a major allergen for those with hay fever. Its leaves are oval in shape, lime green in colour and have serrated edges. The Hazel is a relative of the Alder and the Birch. If it appears in a reading with these other two, it adds extra gravitas to their meanings.

The letter value for Coll / Hazel is a hard 'C', in other words a 'K'. There is no soft 'C' in Gaelic. So, if you want to work with the Ogham for writing or sigil work, you may prefer to use Coll / Hazel for those hard 'C's that sound like 'K's and Saille / Willow for those soft 'C's that sound like 'S's.

The Hazel though is probably best known for its nuts, the Hazelnut, which is much loved by squirrels and humans alike. Hazelnuts, as well as being a great source of nutrients, have long been carried as talisman for wisdom, love, luck and protection from evil of any kind. The nuts tend to ripen quite early and are ready to eat by late August or the start of September, the time of the Hazel in *The Celtic Tree Calendar*.

In Celtic legends its nuts are literally the food of the Gods and were believed to grant anyone who ate them the wisdom and inspiration of the Hazel. According to Irish mythology there once was a pool around which nine Hazel trees grew. Every Autumn their nuts would fall into the pool and be eaten by a salmon who dwelt there and so the salmon was granted great wisdom. The Druid Finegas found out about this and spent seven years fishing for the salmon so he could attain its knowledge. When Finegas eventually caught the salmon, he gave it to his servant Fionn, telling him to cook it but not eat it under any circumstances. Fionn cooked the salmon until he thought it was done and to check it, he touched it with his thumb, which is not a very clever idea. Of course, Fionn burnt his thumb and to ease the burn immediately stuck his thumb into his mouth. In that moment he gained the wisdom of the salmon.[61] From that day forth, Fionn could call upon the wisdom of the salmon simply by biting his thumb, and it was this wisdom, as well as Fionn's courage, that enabled him to become the leader of the Fianna and one of the greatest heroes of Irish legend.

The Hazel symbolises the inspiration that leads to great wisdom. It is the kind of inspiration that has led to the development of both the arts and the sciences. It is the inspiration or muse of the poet and artist and that inspiration or Eureka moment that leads to that incredible moment of understanding or of great scientific discoveries, such as those behind Archimedes' Principle, Einstein's Theory of Relativity or Dmitri Mendeleev's dream in which he created the Periodic Table. Hazel is a catalyst for great things.

Hazel encourages us to bring our dreams into reality. To vision quest and to seek inspiration. When Hazel is cast it shows a time of great inspiration and the learning of important knowledge that will help you, and could even help others, in the long term. This could indicate something like going back to school, researching a new area of interest, taking a class to learn a new skill or honing an existing one, being inspired to create a work of art, being inspired to write, undertaking an apprenticeship or becoming a mentor or teacher. Hazel encourages us to seek advice from elders or those with more experience and skills than we currently have in order to learn from them. It portends great insights. Whatever form this inspiration and learning takes it will open your mind and fill you with new ideas. It will also be surprisingly enjoyable.

Hazel is a keeper of traditional wisdom so can be advising you to look for your answer in legends or lore. It may also be telling you that to find the answer you need to think things through for longer, to ponder, evaluate and await that moment of inspiration. If advice or information is coming your way and you are not sure of it, Hazel tells you to go to the original source, to check any facts, figures or other information for yourself. The last thing you want is to make a major mistake because you failed to check a small, but important detail, or the original message was lost in translation. If you are consulting the Ogham about a decision you need to make, Hazel is advising you in no uncertain terms to use your head and not your heart this time and to think before you act.

The Hazel is also a tree of luck. The Brothers Grimm recorded a version of *Cinderella* where Cinderella plants a Hazel branch on her mother's grave that grows into a tree which is frequented by birds who grant Cinderella wishes.[62] In Wales pliable twigs of Hazel were woven into a special wishing hat that was reputed to grant the wishes of its wearer.[63]

If you are feeling a little stuck, Hazel suggests shaking things up: change your daily routine, explore new things and seek inspiration in new and unusual places. As the twigs of the Hazel are pliant, this tree encourages you to be flexible and adaptable.

The Hazel is often coppiced to encourage it to send out shoots that can be harvested in future for making things like dowsing rods, walking sticks, fencing, baskets and the frames of coracles. It was used to make the rods that were used to protect cattle from fairies and witches or to beat the bounds – a tradition still practiced today where people go around thwacking boundary stones to free them from overgrowing vegetation and make sure they are still where they are supposed to be.[64] Traditionally Y-shaped dowsing rods, especially those used for finding water, are made from Hazel. This is because of the Hazel's natural affinity with the element of water and its alleged ability to increase our natural intuition. The flowing properties of inspiration, intuition and water are very similar.

Hazel was a popular wood for wands, especially for those seeking wisdom or inspiration. Oenghus – the Irish God of Youth and Inspiration was inspired to craft his wand from Hazel.[65] Other deities associated with the Hazel include the Pan-Celtic Goddess of Inspiration and Healing, Brighid, and the Celtic Sea God Manannan Mac Lir who had a special shield made from a withered Hazel tree.[66] It is also the tree of Canola – the Irish Goddess of Music and Inspiration who created the first harp. In the Art Ogham this Few is that of *cruiteacht* or 'harping'.[67]

Coll Reversed

When reversed, Hazel implies a misunderstanding that needs to be resolved quickly and efficiently. Alternately, Hazel implies a creative block or some kind of blockage in your search for wisdom and inspiration. The solution could be to stop overthinking things, to get out of your own head for a bit and to simply sit down and create something, anything, to get the creativity and inspiration flowing again. Perhaps you are feeling disillusioned or your quest for wisdom felt like it was sending you around in circles like a fish in a pond rather than leading you anywhere. Here Hazel tells you to keep going in your quest because, although it may not feel like it, you are making good progress and will get there in the end.

Quert – Apple

Letter: CU
Original Meaning: Apple Tree
Keywords: Health, Healing, Love, Magic
Tree Type in Brehon Laws: Chieftain
Celtic Tree Calendar: Sep 2nd – Sep 29th
Element: Water
Deity: Ceridwen, Morgan le Fay, Abellio, Maponus, Oenghus
Bird Ogham: Hen
Colour Ogham: Mouse-Coloured
Other Colour: Green
People Ogham: Five Women
Crystal: Aventurine
Planet: Venus

Word Oghams
Cuchulainn: *'Excellent emblem (talisman), protection.'*
Oenghus: *'Force of the man.'*
Morann Mac Main: *'Shelter of a lunatic.'*

General Explanation
The Apple is a deciduous tree often found in orchards, hedgerows and gardens. It is one of the Rose family. The leaves are a mid to dark green, oval in shape and are alternatively arranged. Its fruits may be green, red, golden or a combination of all three and these make the tree easy to find in Autumn. September, the time ruled

by the Apple in *The Celtic Tree Calendar*, is usually considered the best time to pick the fruit. In Spring the Apple tree explodes with pale pinkish-white flowers that smell divine. As the flowers have five petals in the shape of a pentagram and the pips, when the fruit is cut in half display the shape of a pentagram, the Apple is considered a tree of the Goddess and of magic.

According to Welsh legend the Apple tree is associated with the Isle of Avalon, the Otherworldly land of Youth and Immortality where Morgan le Fay takes Arthur for healing after he is mortally wounded. *Avalon* means 'The Isle of Apples'.[68] The apple was said to be the food of the Gods in both Celtic and Norse legend and the means by which they stayed youthful. Due to this, it can be associated with Gods of Youth such as Oenghus and Maponus.

Morgan le Fay was rumoured to have a wand carved from the wood of an Avalonian Apple tree. In some more recent versions of the Welsh myths, the Apple tree is associated with the Goddess Ceridwen who is said to guard the Tree of Knowledge in the form of a dragon, while the essence of three sacred apples growing on that tree became three drops of awen or inspiration that fell from Ceridwen's cauldron. In the story of Ceridwen and Taliesin, Ceridwen transforms herself into a hen as she pursues Gwion Bach.[69] She eats him in the form of a grain of corn before giving birth to him, as Taliesin the Bard, nine and a half months later.

The Apple is also linked to the Otherworld or Fairyland in Irish legend. One of the many different names for this realm is *Eamhain Ablach* meaning 'Realm of Apples'.[70] The Irish Sea Deity Manannan Mac Lir had a silver branch from which hung three golden apples that made sweet, healing music and could inspire joy, bring healing or lull a person into a healing sleep.[71] A Gaulish God named Abellio was also associated with the apples that gave him his name.

It is Merlin's connection to the Apple tree that explains *The*

Word Ogham reference to it being *'shelter of a lunatic'*. According to the Mediaeval Welsh poem *Yr Afallennau* ('The Apple Trees') Merlin seeks shelter and protection under the Apples in his divine madness following the defeat of Arthur and the British at the hands of the Saxons.[72] The madness of Merlin is deeply connected to the Celtic idea of inspiration, where the state of creativity is viewed as a 'fire in the head' or a divine madness, from which beautiful works of art or great prophecies are borne, like fruit from the tree. If you have ever been truly touched by inspiration and had that urge to get it out of your head, to stay up all night and forego food, sleep and everything else just to get it done because you wanted and needed to, then you too have experienced this divine inspiration or madness that the Celts believed was borne from the Apple. If you think about it, while apples may not really grant us immortality, creative works can and do give great artists, composers, poets and writers a kind of immortality as their works are appreciated long after they have left this mortal realm.

The Apple bears an incredible amount of fruit and so is seen as a tree of fertility as well as creativity. In a reading it suggests growth, development, fertility, lots of new ideas and a time of things coming to fruition. It is an opportune time to plant new seeds, new ideas, to tend those projects which you already have on the go and to harvest anything that is at the point of completion. The Apple has a bit of a wild reputation and so warns you to just let things happen naturally, rather than trying to wrestle control of the situation, because frankly there is no way you can control it, all you will do is waste a lot of energy and time. Things may all seem a little crazy and wild at the moment, but Apple assures you it is all good.

Today the apple is known for its health-giving properties, hence the phrase *'An apple a day keeps the Doctor away.'* It represents our vigour and life force. When Apple is found in a reading, it is advising you to take good care of your health.

It could be advising you to exercise more, to change your diet, or to look at supplementing your diet with any vitamins or nutrients that you may be in need of.

In divination the Apple refers to a time of healing, rest and recuperation. It could be advising you to take some time out for yourself to restore your energy levels, or indicate that you still have some healing to do after an illness or upset. Apple helps you to find peace in your heart, through the giving and receiving of love – even it is only a bit of self-love. As a tree of beauty Apple calls upon you to witness and appreciate the incredible beauty of the world around you, the beauty of other people's creative outpourings such as poetry and paintings, the innate beauty of other people and your own beauty for you too are beautiful. Apple is a wonderful ally to those with a poor self-image, low self-esteem or low confidence, to learn to love and appreciate themselves.

As a tree of magic, the Apple is often used in various forms of divination. There is a common Halloween custom – still practiced today – that involves peeling an apple in one long strip, then throwing the skin over your shoulder. The pattern it forms is supposed to be the first initial of your future partner's name. Another version is alleged to tell you whether the object of your affection returns your feelings. All you need to do is toss apple pips in to a fire at Halloween and observe their reaction whilst reciting *'If you love me, pop and fly. If you hate me, lay and die.'*[73]

To the Druids of old the Apple was sacred, as it is the most common host tree for their much loved and revered mistletoe. In folk magic parts of the Apple have long been carried as talismans for love, fertility, protection and healing. The Apple is also considered to be a very powerful emblem; it is still used today as an emblem by the Clan Lamont. Druids, Ovates and Bards carried apple branches hung with bells of either gold, silver or bronze according to their class as their emblem of office and as a homage to Manannan Mac Lir's magical branch.

Quert Reversed

Apple reversed implies that you are experiencing ill health or struggling to restore yourself to good health after an illness. It suggests a lack of energy and inspiration. Perhaps you feel exhausted by life or by running around after everyone else in your life, such as your partner, kids and colleagues. Apple warns you that you have been too busy caring for others and that you have neglected your own well-being, and that right now you need to make time to care for yourself for once. Seek help with your health; talk to your health practitioner and work with them to restore yourself to good health.

Chapter 9

The Muinn Aicme

Muinn – Bramble

Letter: M
Original Meaning: Neck
Keywords: Healing, Expression, Abundance, Protection
Tree Type in Brehon Laws: Bush
Celtic Tree Calendar: Sep 2nd – Sep 29th
Element: Air / Earth
Deity: Brighid
Bird Ogham: Titmouse
Colour Ogham: Variegated colours
People Ogham: One Young Person
Crystal: Garnet
Planet: Earth

Word Oghams
Cuchulainn: *'Path of the Voice.'*
Oenghus: *'Condition of slaughter.'*
Morann Mac Main: *'Strongest of effort.'*

General Explanation
Originally Muinn referred to the neck or upper part of the

back of a person or beast. It is that part of us that is rather vulnerable to damage or attack. A strike or blow to the neck can easily be fatal, especially in combat, which is why Oenghus refers to it as *'Condition of slaughter'*. When we exert ourselves the muscles in our neck stand out hence the reference to *'Strongest of effort'*. Our neck is also the path of our voice and gets quite animated when we speak, especially for those with an Adam's apple.

By around the tenth century CE, like the other Fews of the Ogham, Muinn had been assigned a tree and from then on has been associated with the Vine or Bramble. Vines are any technically any plant that climbs or trails, although in Britain and Ireland the term is usually used only to refer to Grapevines. However, the Vine was not indigenous to either Britain or Ireland, although the Ancient British and Irish did trade for wine from the Romans and others and the Romans brought the Vine with them when they invaded Britain. Today many people instinctually feel that Muinn in fact refers not to the Grapevine, but to the Bramble which is native to Ireland and Britain and rich in local lore. Its blackberries were also used to make wine, just like grapes. The truth is we cannot be exactly sure which plant the Vine here refers to because the historical record is not clear and in fact is confusing, because there is a reference to mead – which is made from honey – rather than wine being made from whatever plant the author of *The Ogham Tract* thought the Vine was referring to. For this book, I have decided to work with Muinn as the Bramble because of its rich lore, the fact that there is such a thing as traditional Bramble mead and because in many ways it works with the descriptions of *The Word Oghams*.

Brambles were sacred to the Druids, the Goddess and the fairies, one old byname was 'The Blessed Bramble'.[74] Brambles are part of the Rose family, hence their delicate and pretty flowers, the shapes of their leaves and the dastardly yet wonderfully protective thorns. Oenghus' description of *'Condition of slaughter'* for this Few can just as easily apply to the damage done by Bramble thorns as can Morann Mac Main's *'Strongest of effort'*, as anyone who has ever had to deal with trimming or traversing close to a Bramble will tell you it requires a lot of willpower, effort and inner strength.

In *The Celtic Tree Calendar*, the Bramble rules the bulk of September, the month when its blackberries are ripe for the picking and eating. However, as even those people who know nothing of the ways of witchcraft, folklore or country tales will tell you, you must not eat its berries after Michaelmas on the 29th of September as the fairies will have pissed on them and turned them sour.[75] There is an element of truth to this superstition as the berries do indeed tend to turn sour around the end of September; the conditions in late Autumn result in increased tannin within the berry and encourage a slightly toxic and very foul-tasting mould to grow on the berry.

Bramble is a very protective plant and the thorns and leaves, which also have small thorns on their undersides, are often used in spells for banishing and protection, especially against negative energies, negative entities and our own negative thoughts and behaviours. When Bramble is cast it is recommending that you look to protecting yourself, from those negative parts of yourself as much from the negativity of others. It is a great time to perform some protective magic or strengthen any wards you already have in place. Bramble cautions you to look for any signs of depression, self-destructive tendencies or negative attitudes that are holding you back or blocking your path. Sometimes we truly can be our own worst enemy.

Bramble may suggest that things are getting somewhat prickly right now, perhaps it is your mood, the mood of someone close to you or the situation you are asking about has turned somewhat prickly. Examine why this may have happened, is someone feeling vulnerable, irritated, grumpy or being defensive? Resolve this by talking openly with others. Everyone involved needs the time and space to express themselves and get things off their chest. This is a good time for talking things though with others. It will bring you closer together and strengthen your bonds.

In folk medicine the Bramble is much revered for its incredible healing and beneficial properties. The Bramble speaks to us of healing and good health. It reminds us to eat healthily, to nourish our mind, body and soul. The berries themselves are a superfood like all berries. Just ten berries count as one of your five a day and they are rich in many important nutrients as well as very tasty. Blackberry jams and juices have long been eaten to help with colds, arthritis, and digestive complaints. Its berries and leaves are infamous for being allegedly one of the most soothing and effective treatments for coughs, colds, congestion, bronchitis, laryngitis and other respiratory ailments that affect the voice, which aptly suits Cuchulainn's description of Muinn as *'Path of the Voice'*. The Bramble is sacred to Brighid, the Celtic Triple Goddess of Healing, Poetry and Smithcraft[76] and she is invoked in a traditional healing spell or charm to treat any kind of inflammation which uses Bramble leaves. A poultice is made from leaves and placed on the inflamed area while this phrase is recited: *'Three ladies came from the east; One with fire and two with frost; Out with fire, in with frost.'*

The Bramble is an important plant for British hedgerows, but can also be found on wasteland, in woodlands and in gardens. Brambles can grow pretty much anywhere, are easily grown from seed or by propagation, and will grow very, very fast once established. They also produce a very abundant crop of berries each Autumn and blackberry picking is still a very much-loved tradition. Those gorgeous big berries that we think of as a single berry is in fact lots of tiny berries clumped together. Unusually the Bramble is one of the few plants that can have flowers, leaves and berries all at the same time. This is why the Bramble has long been thought of as a plant of fertility and abundance. With its protective aspect many pagans like to work with the Bramble to protect and grow their wealth. Here the Bramble advises you to look to your finances and personal wealth. It encourages us to grow our wealth in a healthy way, to save for a rainy day, to invest and above all to protect what we have got.

Bramble warns us that there are many who wish to steal away other people's hard-earned cash to line their own pockets, especially today where online fraud is such a common problem. Bramble teaches us to be savvy with our money, not to fall for get rich schemes or email phishing. It also strongly encourages us to make our own money in an honest way and not to scam others. The Bramble also likes to convey to us how rich we all are, even if our bank account says otherwise, for each and every day we get to appreciate the bounty and treasure gifted to us by Mother Nature, just as the Bramble gifts us her valuable fruit come Autumn.

Bramble Reversed

When reversed the Bramble suggests loss, loss of wealth, loss of good health, and a lack of luck, but you can work with the Bramble to turn this around. It warns you that you are getting greedy and advises you to seek only your fair reward. If you do not heed this message, and carry on with your greed and excess, the Bramble will ensure that you regret it, just as eating too many berries will give you stomach ache. May show that you are feeling jealous towards others, especially those you perceive as having more than you. Bramble says stop wasting your energy on being envious and start using that energy to create your own abundance.

Gort – Ivy

Letter: G
Original Meaning: Field
Keywords: Restriction, Binding, Tenacity, Growth, Protection
Celtic Tree Calendar: Sep 30th – Oct 27th
Element: Air
Deity: Arianrhod
Bird Ogham: Swan
Colour Ogham: Blue
People Ogham: Two Young People
Crystal: Opal
Planet: Moon

Word Oghams
Cuchulainn: *'Pleasing oil, corn.'*
Oenghus: *'Size of a warrior.'*
Morann Mac Main: *'Greenest of pasture, sweeter than any grass, ivy…cornfield.'*

General Explanation
Originally Gort referred to a field, an open space in which crops are grown for food or pasture is grown for animals to graze upon. It therefore, represented wealth, abundance and sustenance. In modern Celtic languages its derivatives refer to fields, orchards, crops and enclosures. By around the tenth century CE Gort had come to mean the Ivy. In more recent times this Few has become

associated with the idea of restriction and binding. Fields are often separated by hedgerows and Ivy grows freely in such places. Personally, I have a feeling, and that is all it is, there is no historical justification at all, that how you look at Gort is rather like how you look at a glass with water up to the halfway mark. Is a field a wide, open space, or is it an enclosed, confined space?

The Ivy is an evergreen and woody plant that can be found in forests, hedgerows, gardens and even indoors as a houseplant since it was revealed to be one of the best plants for cleaning the air of certain toxins - NASA's 1989 Clean Air Study.[77] According to folklore, whether it is grown indoors or out, the Ivy brings protection to the home and its occupants.

Ivy may grow low as a creeping plant along the ground never growing more than about twenty-five centimetres high or, where it finds suitable vertical support such as trees or walls, it will become a climbing plant that can reach around thirty metres high. The flowers of the Ivy are greenish-yellow and blossom during late September and October – the time ruled by Ivy in *The Celtic Tree Calendar*. The fruit is a greenish-black with anywhere between one and five seeds. These both provide an important food source for birds and bugs at times of year when there is not much else around for them to eat. So, the Ivy, like other evergreens, symbolises hope, life, fertility and bounty, even in the adversity of winter. Ivy says never give up and never lose hope.

As an extremely tenacious plant, Ivy implies that we too must be resolute, brave and determined at this time. It indicates a challenge that will stretch you to your limit. Can be a warning against any kind of entanglement, especially romantic ones. Also, a forewarning to avoid potential threats or traps. You may be feeling suffocated by current circumstances. An outside force is about to try and exploit or constrain you. If this is a person, be wary of them; they only care about themselves, so steer clear if you can. If it is a situation, then once in it you will find it extremely difficult to extricate yourself and it will have a lingering impact. Ivy can lend its power to restrictive or binding magic and therefore, help protect you, but it can also indicate that you will feel bound or restricted. There is good reason one old country name of the Ivy is Bindwood.[78]

The Ivy speaks to us of our survival instinct and the inner strength that we may not even know that we have. The Ivy implies that your mettle is currently being tested, Oenghus did describe this Few as the *'Size of Warrior'*. This testing time will enable you to grow, particularly in terms of your spirituality.

The Ivy has two leaf shapes, the lobed juvenile stems which grow or creep and the unlobed adult leaves that produce the flowers and berries. It is reputed to both protect the buildings it grows upon as it provides insulation and also to cause them damage with its aerial roots. As a result, the Ivy reminds us that there are two sides to everything and that to truly understand we must listen to and examine both sides before making any decisions or taking action. Ivy also warns us against duplicity; either you are being deceitful with others or someone is being dishonest with you.

Despite it being everywhere, Ivy remains a very mysterious and otherworldly plant. Anywhere it grows seems to have a very ethereal atmosphere. The five lobes of the leaves on the juvenile stems, which have become the equivalent of the classic pentagram for some modern green witches, and the five petals of its flowers indicate that the Ivy is a plant of the Goddess, in her guise as the Goddess of Life, Death and Rebirth. To the Celts, as to the Ancient Egyptians, the Ivy, with its cyclical growth pattern, embodied the cycle of life, death and rebirth, the cyclical movements of the Stars in the firmament above and the cycle of the Moon. In the Midwinter tale of the Holly and the Ivy, the Holly is the Sun God and the Ivy is the Moon Goddess. It is, therefore, no surprise that the Celts associated the Ivy with their Goddess of the Moon, Stars and Fate, Arianrhod, whose name means 'silver wheel' in reference to either the Moon or the circling Stars.

When Ivy appears in a reading it tells you to look up to seek your answers, for they will be found in the magic of the Stars, the Cosmos and the divine. You may like to read your horoscope, or try harmonising your magical work or gardening with the phases of the Moon. Ivy provides us access to the mysteries of the Cosmos. Ivy is also the plant of our dreams and visions. Ivy leaves were placed under the pillow in times past to aid dreaming and dream recall. You can work with the Ivy for vision questing or to bring your dreams into reality. Ivy asks you what your dreams are telling you and advises you to play close attention to them. Ivy also wishes to know what are your dreams for the future and how you plan on living them.

This Few is linked to the swan in the Bird Ogham.[79] Throughout Europe it was believed that the swan was an Otherworldly animal who travelled to the Otherworld when it left our shores on its migration. There was also a common belief that swans carried the souls of the dead from this world to the next.

Traditionally Ivy was a plant of love, symbolising fidelity and the idea of uniting two people together in love. An old English name for Ivy was Lovestone[80] and it has long been carried by young people for vitality, fertility and luck. In some versions of the tragic love story of Tristan and Isolde, after their deaths King Mark placed them in two separate graves to keep the two lovers apart even in death. However, an Ivy grew out from each grave which then met and twined together so the two can finally be connected.[81]

With its ties to the cycles of life, the Ivy is a plant of divination, enhancing your ability to see the patterns and themes in your readings and in the Universe around you. There was a traditional form of divination involving the Ivy that was undertaken at New Year. An Ivy leaf would be placed in water on New Year's Day, and if it was still fresh and green on Twelfth

Night then the year ahead would be blessed with good fortune, however if the leaf shrivelled or went brown, then it portended a year of ill luck. So, Ivy can be telling you to look to your luck and your Karma.

Gort Reversed

When Ivy is reversed it suggests that you are being inconsiderate of others or that you are being selfish. A warning to stop navel-gazing. It calls upon you think of others and the wider picture rather than to just focus on yourself. Ivy reversed cautions you against living in dreamland or wasting energy on pipe dreams that can never come to fruition. How are you currently limiting or restricting yourself with your own thoughts and behaviours? It may also indicate that you and your actions are restricting or suffocating others and preventing them from doing what they need to do.

Ngeadal – Broom

Letter: NG
Original Meaning: Wounding
Keywords: Healing, Cleansing, Calming, Harmony
Tree Type in Brehon Laws: Bush
Celtic Tree Calendar: October 28th – Nov 24th
Element: Water
Deity: Gwydion, Blodeuwedd, Brigid, Airmid, Belenos, Nodens
Bird Ogham: Goose

Colour Ogham: Green
People Ogham: Three Young People
Crystal: Aquamarine
Planet: Sun / Moon

Word Oghams

Cuchulainn: *'Beginning of heroic deeds, healing.'*
Oenghus: *'Robe of Physicians.'*
Morann Mac Main: *'A physician's strength, panacea.'*

General Explanation

The original meaning of this Few was wounding or stabbing, but over time it came to be associated with healing and then later became either the Broom or Reed, depending on who you ask. In this book I'll be taking you through Ngeadal as the Broom because that is how it was listed in *The Ogham Tract* which dates back to the fourteenth century CE. You may be wondering quite what wounding and healing have in common, but it is not until we are hurt or ill that we tend to consult our doctor and a doctor does not get to utilise their skills until we are at their door in pain.

The Broom of the Ogham is the Common Broom, Scottish Broom or *Cytisus scoparius* to give it its official name. It can be found growing in grasslands, shrublands and woodlands. Generally, it likes a dry, sunny spot and a sandy, acidic soil. The Broom is deciduous and grows to around two to three metres tall. It has ridged, dark green stems and small trifoliate leaves. In Spring and Summer, it is easy to find because it is absolutely covered in golden flowers that smell very strongly of Vanilla. Come late Summer it produces seed pods which darken throughout the Autumn before bursting open to spread their seeds come November, the time ruled by Broom in *The Celtic Tree Calendar*.

The Broom is technically a legume rather than a tree and

is a relative of the Gorse. Like other legumes it is a nitrogen fixer thanks to its symbiotic relationship with the Rhizobium bacteria. Effectively this means that the Broom heals and enhances the soil it grows in rather than exhausting it. Broom itself is a healer and for centuries was beloved by healers for its many medicinal properties. Traditionally it was considered a *panacea* or 'heal-all' and used to treat arthritis, bone and muscle pains, water retention, liver and lung complaints, palpitations, irregular heartbeats or rapid beating of the heart and to increase blood pressure.[82] Modern science has acknowledged its medicinal properties, but with a warning, for it is in fact so powerful that it is toxic unless used by top notch experts who know exactly what they are doing. There is a fine line between healing and harm as most doctors know, as indeed does anyone who has ever had a serious reaction to a herb or medication. So, it is easy to understand why this Few refers to both harming and healing. In modern medicine Sparteine, which the plant contains, is sometimes used as a cardiac stimulant and is considered superior to digoxin, yet it also has the potential of causing a heart attack.

As a plant with such amazing healing properties, it is considered sacred to the Celtic Deities of Healing such as Brighid, Airmid, Belenos and Nodens. The Broom is best known though in Celtic mythology as one of the flowers that Gwydion used to create the woman of flowers – Blodeuwedd, the Welsh Goddess of Spring.[83]

Because of the strong scent of its flowers, today many view the this Few as that of aromatherapy – the therapeutic use of essential oils to promote well-being. Broom may be asking you to literally stop and smell the flowers and plants. Perhaps try utilising aromatherapy or using scent in your home or on your person in the form of oils, incense, fresh flowers or perfumes to promote a sense of healing and calm harmony. Scent is powerful; it can provoke memories, improve our memory and change our mood. According to old country lore the scent of Broom is so calming that it could tame wild horses and dogs.[84]

Broom can also be telling you to clean up because things have become unpleasant, dirty or the energies have become stagnant. It is no coincidence that the common name for this plant in English is the same for the domestic tool used to sweep away dust and detritus for the twigs of the Broom were often used to make the bristles of the besom. In the past the wings of the goose were also used to sweep up dust,[85] so could go further to explain the connection between this Few and the goose.

Broom is advising us to clear up our own mess. The situation that we currently find ourselves in is essentially our own mess and now it is down to us to get ourselves out of it. Broom may be advising you to have a really good clear out and tidy up – physically, emotionally and spiritually. Clear out all that is no longer helping you, that is holding you back, or feels stagnant and yucky. Shed the baggage of the past; learn from it and move on. Make way for positive bright, fresh new, energies to enter your life. Sometimes we fear letting go, preferring to cling on to the familiar, but Broom shows us how healing and liberating letting go can be.

The Celtic month of the Broom falls at the end of the old Celtic year when traditionally people took stock, cleared out the old and made way for the new. When Broom appears in a reading alongside Birch, which symbolises fresh new starts and Spring cleaning, it is really pushing this aspect home to you.

The cleansing energy of Broom is not just about cleansing the physical; it also reminds us to cleanse our auras, for just as our homes accumulate dust, our auras accumulate energies from the places we go, the people we meet and the things we come in contact with.

It may indicate the need for purification and protection.

Witches have long used their broom or besom as a magical tool of protection, many witches – past and present – symbolically place a broom by their door to protect their home from negative energies. Ironically in some parts of the world doing this was actually said to prevent witches from entering the house.[86] If you choose a besom made with fresh Broom, be sure not to cut it just before the plant is due to flower, for there is a superstition that should you sweep your home with Broom in flower, especially in the month of May, you will sweep away the head of the household.[87]

Because of its symbiotic relationship with Rhizobium, the Broom is a symbol of harmony; harmony between you and the others in your life, harmony between your work life and home life, harmony between your head and your heart, harmony between you and the planet and harmony between this realm and the otherworld. When Broom appears it is telling you in no uncertain terms that you need to get your life and yourself back in balance. This is where you will find peace and healing.

Ngeadal Reversed

When reversed Broom infers illness or unease. This does not necessarily mean an ailment, rather it warns you to take care of yourself and tend to your health and sense of well-being. It warns you not to get downhearted, even if you are unwell or suffering in any way because its bright flowers and heavenly scent cheer the heart and soul. As well as consulting your physician, Broom asks you to look to nature to heal yourself, take a walk in a park, a woodland or other green space to heal your soul and find peace. Green is after all the colour of nature, harmony, healing and the heart chakra. Broom wants you to be happy and encourages you to look for the simple things in life that can make you happy. Look after yourself.

Straif – Blackthorn

Letter: STR
Original Meaning: Sulphur
Keywords: Strife, Negativity, Pain, Conflicts
Tree Type in Brehon Laws: Lower Division
Celtic Tree Calendar: Samhain (from sunset on Oct 31st – to sunset Nov 1st)
Element: Air / Fire
Deity: The Cailleach / Morrigan
Bird Ogham: Thrush
Other Animals: Wolf, Black Cat, Toad
Colour Ogham: Bright
People Ogham: Four Young People
Crystal: Jet
Planet: Saturn / Mars

Word Oghams
Cuchulainn: *'The mist of an arrow, smoke from a fire.'*
Oenghus: *'Increasing of secrets, sloe.'*
Morann Mac Main: *'Strongest of red. Dye.'*

General Explanation
Judging by the etymology, Straif once referred to Sulphur, a mineral that is both deadly to life and necessary for life, which is quite an astounding contradiction. In Mediaeval times Sulphur was sometimes known by the rather eldritch name of Brimstone.

To the alchemists it made a panacea and could be used in the process of transforming base metals into gold.[88] On the other hand, Hell was supposed to be full of fire and brimstone, and so the Devil, witches and any kind of evil apparently reeked of it. Some say the smell of sulphur deterred witches,[89] others said it drew them to it like moths to a flame. Today we still use a form of sulphur in some skin creams and for matches. It is literally what ignites the match and so fits well with Cuchulainn's *Word Ogham*. Traditionally Sulphur was used to make dyes, but interestingly it cannot be used to make red dyes so cannot be what Morann Mac Main describes.

Over time, when the Fews were being assigned trees, Straif came to mean the Blackthorn. It is clear that this tree is what Oenghus is talking about this tree because he talks of its fruit, the sloe. The sloe makes a dye that initially turns cloth red before then washing out to a pale blue and the bark of the Blackthorn makes a red-brown dye so could well be what Morann Mac Main was describing.

The Blackthorn is a shrub that tends to be found in hedgerows, woodlands and some wastelands. Blackthorn is an important ally to the hedge witch who seeks to understand the secrets of the Universe. With age the Blackthorn becomes beautiful gnarled and twisted, shaped by fate and the elements, but never losing its identity or power and so offers us a very powerful lesson that while we may be shaped by fate, by circumstances and by age, we never lose the inner core of who we are. Those lines we have on our faces, we earned those and should wear them proudly. To be able to grow old is a blessing, many do not get the chance and so while we may moan and groan about what age does to our bodies, we should also think how very lucky we are to still be alive.

The Blackthorn is often found growing close to its sister, the Hawthorn, who is sometimes called the Whitethorn to emphasise their sisterhood and how they are like opposite sides of the same coin. As with the Oak and Holly Kings there is an idea that the Blackthorn and Hawthorn each rule over half of the year. The time when the Hawthorn is Queen runs from Beltane at the start of Summer to Samhain. The Blackthorn rules from Samhain to Beltane. This explains why in *The Celtic Tree Calendar* the Blackthorn is said to rule over the Celtic Festival of Samhain.

With its five petalled flowers, so reminiscent of the Pentagram, the Blackthorn is a tree of magic and the Goddess in her darker forms. It is one of the Trees of The Irish Goddess of Fate and War, The Morrighan. According to Scottish folklore at Samhain the Hag of Winter – The Cailleach blasts all life with her magical rod of Blackthorn and so the vegetation dies back.[90] Worry not, for come Spring Brighid will return and restore life again with her Birch rod. It is all just part of the cycle of life, death and rebirth. The power of Blackthorn is, therefore, transformation. While most of the time we do have the power to change our circumstances, Blackthorn suggests that either we cannot change them in this particular instance or that what we really need to do is to change our own attitude to what is happening. Will you accept this challenge?

Samhain is a Festival of the Dead and a time when the veil between this world and the next is so thin as to be almost non-existent. This is what makes it such an opportune time for magic, divination and spiritual work. Samhain marks the beginning of Winter, when we find ourselves spending more time indoors and more time going within ourselves, to meditate, to practice divination, to work with the ancestors, to practice magic and to work on our inner selves. This is a very important part of Blackthorn's message to us. While Blackthorn seems to have brought complete chaos to your life, that it has brought you is in fact valuable time to transform yourself. Blackthorn advises us to go within, to seek refuge from the worst of Winter or the chaos of current events in the safe and sacred space that is our home, to make it a cosy and warm place where we love to spend time and where we feel we can truly be ourselves and just relax. Blackthorn encourages us to go within ourselves too, to undertake deep contemplation, to find peace with our own company, to find comfort, peace and the answers we seek deep within.

The Blackthorn is traditionally associated with misfortune and detrimental forces. Our modern English word of 'strife' is cognate with Straif. So, we recognise that Blackthorn in a reading can indicate strife, punishment and everything going badly wrong. Plans are going awry, events and people may be getting you down, and you feel as if everything around you has gone completely to pot. Wherever you turn there seems to be uncertainty, negativity and conflicts. Whatever you do you cannot seem to get things back on track, no matter how hard you try. Blackthorn says 'Do not worry, you are not meant to'. Blackthorn is shaking things up completely so that things can be transformed for the future. It is from this chaos that great new things will emerge. Compare it to the seed sprouting in the compost formed from the dead leaves of the previous winter. In the past the ashes from Blackthorn fires were spread on the fields to enhance their fertility.[91] Do not let events get you down or depress you, instead keep your spirits up, focus on the amazing potential that exists right now look forward to that bright new future.

As Winter is a time of dormancy, Blackthorn strongly encourages us to rest and recuperate at this time. Have an early night, catch up on your sleep and get into some good sleep habits. In this crazy fast-paced modern world we all live in, sleep is often the first thing to go to enable us to get done all the things we feel we need to do. Blackthorn tells us to stop, evaluate what is important and ditch the rest so we can get back to getting the rest that we so desperately need. Gather your strength, think things through and make plans, and generally utilise this time to get yourself ready to move forward with confidence when the metaphorical Spring returns.

As the increaser of secrets, Blackthorn urges us to always keep seeking to understand the deep and magical secrets of Mother Nature and the Universe. If we have been entrusted with secrets, Blackthorn tells us to keep them and, if necessary, to take them to our grave. Many witches today, work with Blackthorn to help them to learn more of the magical secrets of the craft and to protect those secrets from those outside the craft. Witches who are still in the broom closet may also chose to work with Blackthorn to help protect and keep their chosen spiritual path, and their tools, hidden from prying eyes.

Blackthorn helps us to get through difficult times and overcome challenges we may encounter, no matter how harsh or hard they may appear. The flowering of the Blackthorn is a magical and blessed sight and rebirth after the death and darkness of winter. It reminds us of hope, of the light in the darkness, of the light of the Stars that guide our way, the light at the end of the tunnel and of nature's power of transformation.

Straif Reversed

Many consider this Few, when reversed, to be the most sombre and depressing of all as it suggests death, but that is a bit of a misunderstanding. This can be a literal death, but far more likely this death refers to the cessation or removal of something within a person, say giving up a bad habit, ending a cycle of behaviour or deciding to change your attitude. It can also mean a death as in an ending, say the end of a career or phase of life. All things must end sometime. New life is born from the old. It may very well be painful, so take the time you need to grieve and heal.

Ruis – Elder

Letter: R
Original Meaning: Reddening
Keywords: Karma, Transformation, Regeneration, Renewal, Magic
Tree Type in Brehon Laws: Lower Division
Celtic Tree Calendar: Nov 25th – Dec 21st (the thirteenth Moon)
Element: Fire
Deity: Arianrhod, The Elder Mother
Bird Ogham: Rook
Other Animal: Badger
Colour Ogham: Blood Red
People Ogham: Five Young People
Crystal: Ruby
Planet: Venus

Word Oghams

Cuchulainn: *'A fierce anger, punishment.'*
Oenghus: *'Redness of faces, blushing.'*
Morann Mac Main: *'Intensest of blushes. From the reddening of shame or from rubbing the juice on the face.'*

General Explanation

The Elder is a shrubby tree that absolutely loves to grow wild, for it still has a very wild spirit. It can be found in hedgerows, wastelands, woods, gardens, and even trying to grow in concrete cracks in roads and pavements. Elder grows easily from seed or cutting, even in poor conditions and will still produces masses of flowers and berries, so it has long been seen as a tree of fertility and regeneration.

Its flowers are white, very fragrant and often used to make elderflower wine or cordial. Elderflowers are said in folklore to have an eerie effect on people, producing strange dreams or helping them to see clairvoyantly. The berries are small and black and often used to make jams and cordials. The Druids gathered elderberries to make a special ritual wine that they used to help them cross the threshold of the spiritual worlds and to seek the wisdom of the old Gods and Goddesses of the *Tuatha Dé Danann*.[92] The Elder calls on you to pay attention to your dreams and visions and to seek wisdom from the wise ones.

In folk medicine the Elder is highly prized for its healing properties and has long been used to treat just about every ailment ever known to humankind. Yet it is also poisonous as every part of the Elder contains a form of cyanide. There can be a fine line between life and death and it is at this threshold that the Elder proudly stands. Straif, or the Blackthorn, represented chaos and death, and now it is followed by the Elder which represents that mysterious time after death and before rebirth. The time of the Elder in *The Celtic Tree Calendar* is from October 28th to November 24th, the time of year when everything is dying back. The Elder is also associated with the very similar energy of the waning Moon.

Various parts of the Elder are used to make different dyes, which transform the appearance of cloth. The juice of the berry makes blue and purple dyes, the roots make a black dye and the bark makes a red dye. When cut the Elder tree even appears to bleed red, just as we bleed when injured. In English the words dye and die sound the same and this serves as a powerful reminder that sometimes a part of us must die in order for us, like the cloth, to be transformed or reborn anew.

The wise, old Elder is the ultimate tree of the Goddess: the leaves consist of five leaflets on a stalk, while the flower has five petals, five stamen and five sepals. As the *The Wiccan Rede* explains: *'Elder be ye lady's tree, burn it not or cursed ye'll be.'*[93] In European folklore the Elder tree has a very unique characteristic for many people she is consider her to be a Goddess, Fairy Queen or Guardian Spirit in her own right. She is best known as the Elder Mother, a Crone Goddess who guards the door to the Otherworld, the threshold between life and death who is associated with regeneration, renewal, magic and the dark mysteries. As the Guardian between life and death the Elder is reputed to have the power to repel all kinds of negative energies and entities and, like garlic, was once used to deter vampires, ghosts and the undead.

Generally, the Elder Mother is benevolent and kind, after all she offers us healing in the form of the old folk remedies. Yet she will also viciously punish those who have harmed her, hence the very apt description of this Few as 'A fierce anger, punishment' by Cuchulainn. It was traditional for those who wanted to work with the parts of the Elder to ask first and take a moment to wait for an answer, a feeling, as to whether or not it was OK to proceed. The ritual phrase used still survives today: *'Old girl, give me some of thy wood and I will give thee some of mine when I grow into a tree.'*[94] This is not meant to be morbid; it is simply an exchange of energies. It seems only fair that after death our bodies give back to the very soil and plants that provided sustenance for us. From the old grows the new. Elder trees were sometimes planted by Celts on the graves of their ancestors. When the Elder flowered, they knew that their loved ones had reached the afterlife or been reborn and were thriving there, just as the Elder thrived in this world. It was reassuring.

When Elder is found in a reading it indicates a transition or rite of passage of some kind. This could be a physical trip, a change in health, advancing in your career or spiritual path, or a spiritual journey. It can indicate a very transitory time in life, you may move house, change career or your relationship status may change. If you are experiencing grief or loss, the Elder Mother offers you heartfelt understanding and sympathy. She knows only too well what it is like to lose someone or something dear to you. The Elder Mother asks you to look inside yourself and wonder if you died today what would your regrets be? She bids you to say those things you would regret not saying, especially to your loved ones, and to do those things that you would regret not doing.

She reaffirms the message we encountered with Blackthorn; all things must end, but the wheel of the cycle of life, death and rebirth is always turning like the seasons. In her very gentle manner, she explains that death is simply the movement from one realm of existence to another, a transformation, just like that of the caterpillar to the butterfly. Elder also reminds us that what goes around, comes around. These lessons are also those taught by the Welsh Goddess of Fate, Arianrhod.

The Elder Mother is usually an incredibly kind and approachable Grandmother type who has your best interests at heart as long as you treat her with kindness. She is wise in the ways of Karma and knows absolutely everything about you: she has seen your actions, heard your thoughts and words, and observed how you treat others. She knows all your dirty and embarrassing secrets. Here is where the blushing of *The Word Ogham* for Elder comes in, because we've all done things we sincerely regret, that we ae embarrassed about or ashamed of. Like a mirror, the Elder shows us our past and asks us if this is really the Karmic debt we want hanging over us. If you feel that need to make any changes in light of your answer, the Elder Mother reminds you that you and only you can do this. No one else can do it for you.

If you are looking for answers, drawing Elder suggests that

you need to seek protection and assistance from the divine, from queenly or motherly figures in your life that you can trust. They can offer sound and practical advice from someone who has very likely been though something similar, or knows someone who has. The wisdom and guidance that you will receive will allow you to make positive changes, to turn your life around and to view things in a whole new, fresh and positive way. It may feel like being reborn.

Ruis Reversed

If you are feeling wronged or hard done by, Elder reminds you that the situation you are in is ultimately of your own making. Fate and Karma is settling debts with you. It could well be humiliating or shameful for you. You cannot escape this, rather you need to take it all on board, learn from it and do better in future. In order to change the status quo, you are going to have to do some very deep soul searching and make some serious changes, but Elder reassures you that you do have the power to transform and renew yourself and your Karma.

Chapter 10

The Ailm Aicme

Ailm – Pine

Letter: A
Original Meaning: The 'Ah' Sound
Keywords: Expression, Purification, Perception, Enlightenment
Tree Type in Brehon Laws: Chieftain
Celtic Tree Calendar: Dec 23rd (Yule)
Element: Fire
Deity: Druantia, Ogma
Bird Ogham: Lapwing
Other Animal: Phoenix
Colour Ogham: Piebald
Other Colour: Gold
People Ogham: One Child
Crystal: Gold / Amber
Planet: Sun

Word Oghams & Other Sources
Cuchulainn: *'Beginning of a weaver's beam, ahhh (as in a sound made by a person).'*
Oenghus: *'Beginning of an answer, for the first expression of every human being after his birth is aaaaah.'*

Morann Mac Main: *'Loudest of groanings, that is wondering. For it is the 'ah' a man says while groaning in disease, or wondering, that is, marvelling at whatever circumstance.'*

King Henry & the Hermit (an old Irish poem): *'Beautiful are the pines which make music for me'.*

The Song of Amergin: *'I am the womb of every holt.'*

General Explanation

Although originally referring to just the 'ah' sound, in time Ailm became the Pine tree perhaps because this sound is so similar to the sound that the wind makes as it blows through the needles of the Pines in a forest. After the death of Straif and the profound transition of Ruis, we now encounter that bright and beautiful moment of rebirth with the energies of Ailm – the Pine. Pine encourages us to see the world anew, to gaze upon it with awe and appreciation. Now is the time to learn from those mistakes of the past, to take what we have learned and to apply it to the future. Do not dwell on the past, look forward and get going. Potential problems will shy away from the light you are confidently shining into the world and so, for now, your path is clear.

The Pine of the Ogham is most likely to be what we now call the Scot's Pine, which is indigenous to Ireland, Britain and much of Eurasia. In some Ogham systems you may see it listed as the Silver Fir, but the Silver Fir was not introduced until the seventeenth century CE. Part of the confusion may be down to the fact that the Scot's Pine used to be referred to as a Fir tree or the Scot's Fir.

The Pine is an evergreen Conifer that can grow to a staggering thirty-five metres high. To think that it starts as a little tiny seed and become so majestic just shows how much potential this tree has. Pine encourages us to see that great potential that exists within us and within others and to continue to always grow and develop, particularly in our spirituality, for the Pine reaches far up into the heavens and therefore, gets closer to the divine.

Pines are long lived and can live for a thousand years or so. Although one bristlecone Pine, called Methuselah, is believed to be over 4,800 years old[95] and is one of the oldest living organisms in the world. Their family of trees, Pinus, is also an ancient one as Pines are thought to have evolved around 200 million years ago. It can also highlight that any factors involved in your question are, or will be, longstanding or show you a long-term prediction.

From as far back as the time of the Ancient Egyptians parts of the Pine have been used for healing, as a tonic, an antiseptic, a stimulant and to treat the entire range of respiratory problems. Even walking in a Pine forest was considered to be a healing experience,[96] for their scent was said to heal the soul. Perhaps this is why the Pine essential oil and cleaning products with a Pine scent are so popular today? For generations Pines have symbolised longevity and good health, so whenever you pull this Few, it is a good sign for your health and wellbeing.

As crazy as it may sound the Pine communicates secrets to those who know how to understand them. They tell us how they are doing: how healthy they are and how healthy the soil is in which they are growing. They do this via their candles – the new Spring shoots. It also appears that the Pine is privy to the great secret of the Universe that is the Fibonacci sequence for its cones, needles and branches all tend to follow this very distinct pattern. So, Pine advises you to watch for and listen to messages coming to you from nature.

The Pine is a tree of the Sun and of fire, hence its new shoots being called 'candles'. It is closely associated with the Sun in particular as its cones grow in a spiral pattern following the path of the Sun. Within The Celtic Tree calendar, Pine's time falls on December 23rd at the time when the Sun-child is born, and thus begins the light half of the year. December 23rd is the first day when the length of the day can be seen to be growing after standing still at the Midwinter Solstice. Traditionally the Pine was favoured for making the fiery brands that our ancestors used as torches, and it gives off the most heavenly smell when burnt. In the past fire was thought of as purifying and cleansing, and ritual fires were often burned to dispel negative or stagnant energies and to bless animals and people.[97] The resin of the Pine has long been burned as incense to purify homes and sacred spaces.

In a reading Pine may suggest the need to put a fire under something metaphorically to get things moving, or perhaps you feel that someone has lit a fire under you. Pine suggests things happening quickly, dynamically and suddenly. You may experience inspiration, revelations or bursts of joy or enlightenment as Pine as a metaphorical torch illuminates your situation and allows you to really see what is going on. Here Pine is the light that reveals what has been hidden.

As a tree of perception, Pine asks you to examine your own perception of the issue you are consulting the Ogham about. Are you seeing the full picture or can you not see the wood for the trees? Are you being objective in this situation or is your vision being clouded by your own emotions, expectations or experiences? Because it is such a tall tree, Pine encourages us to get a good overview of things, to stand back and get a broader view. To try to understand where everyone involved in the situation is coming from and how everyone hopes it will develop. The best way to do this is to talk to everyone involved.

Pine is the Few of expression and communication. It is telling you to speak up and speak out. You need to express your opinion and feel heard. Right now, you are feeling a very strong urge to express your truth. Allows others to express their opinions and true selves to you too. Really listen to what others have to say, do not pass judgement, but thank them for their contributions and take what they say on board. When we feel listened to, we feel valued and appreciated. Pine can indicate that you are finally coming out of your shell, or shows that you may need to do so in order to be heard. Pine urges you to stand up, stand tall, be proud of yourself.

Pine asks you what it is that you want to communicate or share to the world. Pine urges you to express yourself. The important thing is to enjoy the process of expression, to let out those pent-up feelings and thoughts so that you can go 'ah' in satisfaction or awe, rather than in pain or frustration. The Pine lifts the spirits, its bright energy chases away despondency and despair so this Few indicates a time of much happiness, fabulous new opportunities and lots of chances to express yourself and feel free.

Pine and the time of the Midwinter Solstice are sacred to the Goddess Druantia[98] – also known as 'The Queen of the Druids'. Although originally an Oak Deity, she has since become linked with the Pine. In modern paganism the Pine is also the tree of the Irish God of Poetry and Expression, Ogma, who the Ogham may be named for.

Ailm Reversed

When reversed the Pine infers that you are feeling very hurt by recent experiences and are not feeling listened to. It may imply that you are either tongue-tied and unable to express yourself properly or conversely that you have been over-sharing or repeating yourself which has resulted in people no longer listening to you. Can also be warning you about divulging too much information to others, especially online, as it can expose you to fraud. After all the name of your first pet or mother's maiden name do tend to be used as security questions. Perhaps you have been giving your opinion where it was not wanted and not asked for. So here the Pine asks you to re-evaluate how you are expressing yourself and to think very carefully before communicating with others.

Onn – Gorse

Letter: O
Original Meaning: Ash Tree
Keywords: Vitality, Abundance, Gathering, Gratitude
Tree Type in Brehon Laws: Bush
Celtic Tree Calendar: Mar 21st (Spring Equinox) & Aug 1st (Lughnasadh)
Element: Air / Fire
Deity: Llew / Lugh
Bird Ogham: Scrat
Other Animals: Hare, Rabbit
Colour Ogham: Dun-Coloured
Other Colour: Yellow
People Ogham: Two Children
Crystal: Citrine
Planet: Sun

Word Oghams & Other Sources
Cuchulainn: *'Strength of a warrior, fierceness.'*
Oenghus: *'Smoothest of work, stone.'*
Morann Mac Main: *'Helper of horses, the wheels of the chariot. Also, equally wounding.*
The Song of Amergin: 'I am the blaze on every hill.'

General Explanation
Onn used to mean the Ash tree, which it now represented by

Nuinn, but now symbolises the Gorse. This explains why *The Word Oghams* refer to war, warriors and chariots for Ash was often used to make spears and chariots. Onn is sometimes listed by modern authors as Furze – Furze and Gorse are two different names for the very same plant, *Ulex europaeus*.

The Gorse is a short-lived evergreen shrub that grows to around three metres tall. It is a tough plant that thrives in low temperatures, yet can also survive intense fires as it can regrow from its roots after a wildfire. It tends to prefer quite sandy, acidic soil, but will grow on shingle and even wasteland. So, Gorse shows us how to thrive – even in some very difficult conditions.

Gorse is a legume and a relative of the Broom. Like the Broom it fixes nitrogen into the soil, helping to replenish and heal it. It is a plant that speaks to us of healing ourselves and looking to our own wellbeing. In the past the Gorse was used as a tonic, an antiseptic, a diuretic, to boost the immune system, to increase blood pressure, as a salve for dry and cracked skin[99] and as a pain reliever for headaches and arthritis. It can however be toxic to humans. That said horses love to eat its tender tips, so Gorse is indeed *'Helper of horses'*.

The leaves are a very deep green, trifoliate and form spines or thorns, so this plant knows how to defend itself. It is as fierce and wounding as Cuchulainn and Morann Mac Main describe. The flowers are bright yellow and have a coconut-vanilla scent. When the Gorse blooms, it does indeed seem to blaze across the hillsides as *The Song of Amergin* describes. The best thing about these flowers is that they can be found for most of the year, although they are at their very best at the time of the Spring Equinox, which is perhaps why the Gorse rules that Festival in *The Celtic Tree Calendar* in some versions.

There is a quaint old piece of folklore that tells us 'When the gorse is out of bloom, kissing is out of fashion,'[100] and so the Gorse has long been associated with love and romance.

Gorse shows the sweetness of your relationship, it is a time of much romance. Once upon a time Gorse was added to bridal bouquets for love and fertility. Make sure you spend time with your partner and shower them with your love.

The Gorse symbolises the abundance of blessings that we are gifted with each and every day, for it seems to provide a bountiful harvest of cheerful golden flowers, the sight of which cannot fail to lift the heart. This is why the Gorse is the ruler of Lughnasadh, the first of the Harvest Festivals in *The Celtic Tree Calendar*. The vibrant yellow flowers of the Gorse symbolise its link to the Sun and to Lugh – the Celtic God of Light. Lughnasadh is after all his festival. In Brittany Lughnasadh is celebrated as *Fête des Fleurs d'Ajoncs* or the 'Gorse Flower Festival'.[101]

Gratitude encourages the kind of positivity and positive thinking that Gorse represents. Gorse encourages us to actively practice gratitude, to be thankful for and appreciative of the amazing blessings we are being gifted with on a daily basis. To be grateful to Mother Earth, the divine, the plants, animals and people who have provided for us. For example, for the food we eat we should be thankful to the plants or animals for their sacrifice, thankful to the earth, water and air that sustained them, to the farmer who watched over them, the person who harvested, packed, transported, warehoused and sold it to us, and to the person who prepared the food for the table, if it was not ourselves. That is an awful lot to be grateful for. Practice true gratitude with actions and words and let the world know how much you appreciate it.

Like the Gorse you too are flowering at the moment. You are filled to bursting with new ideas, plans for the future and lots of energy. This Few indicates a time of plenty – an abundant and profitable time. Plans and undertakings are coming along nicely and opportunities are there for the taking. Life feels so sweet right now. Gorse is a sign of amazingly positive things coming your way, so many in fact that you may not be able to take them all on. If you cannot, it is a great opportunity to help others. You can pass a few of these opportunities onto them and give them chances they may not otherwise have had. Pay it forward and build up some great Karma for when you might need other people in the future.

With this abundance of blessings everywhere in your life, the wise decision is to gather some for the future, especially for those rainy days, or those Winter days when all that abundance of the Summer and the good times seems just a distant memory. Gather what you need, but only what you need. Just as the wisest of foragers knows, you must always leave some for others and enough for plants to be able to regrow or to seed themselves once again, so that you can come back and harvest them year after year. This gathering can refer to saving your pennies, or gathering materials for the future, but it can also mean gathering new skills, gathering information, gathering together with like-minded people to achieve a goal or gathering new contacts that could help you in the future.

Gorse can also suggest that you need to gather yourself together. Perhaps you find yourself faced with a multitude of decisions, maybe you have a million ideas floating around in your head, maybe you are feeling overwhelmed by lots of different emotions or are feeling pulled in a hundred different directions. Whatever it is that is making you feel scattered, take time to collect your thoughts, gather yourself together and focus on your plans for the future.

The Gorse is very much linked to the humble and hardworking bee, as is Ura /Heather. You too have worked hard and are now reaping the rewards of your efforts. Share this bounty with others and everyone will benefit. This is a time when you will achieve recognition for your efforts and feel accomplished. Enjoy the bounty, but also get ready to sow the seeds for the next one.

In a reading Gorse can show the need to add some colour and

inspiration into your life. If you are feeling that life has become boring, Gorse offers you the chance to shake things up with a bit of colour. Try bringing more colour into your wardrobe, change your hair colour, become a plant parent to a colourful new plant, repaint a wall or room in your house or treat yourself to some colourful new furnishings. See how it inspires you. You can add colour in other ways too: change up the food you eat, try eating more of the rainbow, for food come in a whole rainbow of colours. Change your habits; for example, change your route to work so can you can some colourful, interesting and inspiring new things.

As it is almost constantly in flower, and profusely so, the Celts saw the Gorse as perpetually fertile. Today its blooms are still used in love, fertility and prosperity magic. With all this bounty and fertility, no wonder Gorse is associated with the hare and the rabbit. Gorse was sometimes burned in Beltane fires, through which cattle were driven for protection, purification and fertility.[102] With its prickly leaves, the Gorse implies that you need to carefully protect that which you gather.

Gorse is always a positive and encouraging sign; it brings hope, optimism, vitality and the promise of amazing things to come. It is the bright Sun above, the light at the end of the tunnel, our inner flame and the fire of love. Look to the light and do what you need to in order to carefully tend these flames so that they burn bright and you too can be a source of hope, joy and inspiration for others.

Onn Reversed

You have accidentally discovered the less pleasant side of the Gorse: its prickly thorns and its ability to hem in people and cattle. This can lead you to feeling trapped. Avoid getting tangled in risky ventures or other people's problems. Do not be swayed or deterred by others from your plans. Plan things through carefully to achieve your goals. You may be finding that people are being prickly or tetchy with you. Resist the urge to treat them in the same way. Can imply that you are feeling disillusioned or that all your plans are scattering to the four winds. You may feel that the bounty and abundance of the past is slipping away from you. Find your happy place and think positive.'

Ur – Heather

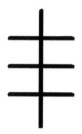

Letter: U
Original Meaning: Moist Soil
Keywords: Love, Passion, Partnership, Luck
Tree Type in Brehon Laws: Bush
Celtic Tree Calendar: June 21st (Summer Solstice)
Element: Fire
Deity: Graine, Anu, Branwen, Uroica
Bird Ogham: Lark
Other Animal: Bee
Colour Ogham: Resinous
Other Colours: Mauve and Red
People Ogham: Three Children
Crystal: Amethyst
Planet: Venus / Mars

Word Oghams & Other Sources
Cuchulainn: 'Completion of lifelessness, the grave.'
Oenghus: 'Growing of plants, heath, the soil of the earth, that which causes the growing of the plants that are put into it.'

Morann Mac Main: *'In cold dwellings. The mould of the earth.'*
The Song of Amergin: *'I am the queen of every hive.'*

General Explanation

In the ancient past it seems that Ur was used to refer to the moist soil in which plants and trees grow. It was the support and sustenance for the forests, crops and healing herbs that our ancestors relied upon for their food, wood, fuel, tools and more. Its health was and still is vital to our own. A poor harvest could mean the difference between life and death in times gone by. We are born from the earth, sustained by it and ultimately it is also the same soil that we give life to when we die, for we become nutrients in the earth that fuels the plants that grow within it for the future.

By the time of *The Ogham Tract*, Ur has become Heather and in the Agricultural Ogham Ur is listed as *usca* or 'heatherbrush'.[103] Heather and the heath and moorland, the lands it grows upon, are synonymous with each other. Heather is the land and the land is Heather, perhaps in part because the plant grows so low to the ground and can fill entire valleys.

The Heather the Ogham refers to is known as Common Heather, Ling or *Calluna Vulgaris*. It is a low-growing and woody evergreen shrub that loves acidic soils. It also tolerates some light grazing from animals and will regenerate well following a fire. At the other end of the scale Heather can survive freezing conditions down well below minus twenty degrees Celsius or minus four degrees Fahrenheit, so Heather teaches us to be hardy and to thrive and be joyful, even in inhospitable and chilly circumstances.

As Calluna vulgaris it takes its name from the ancient Greek word καλλύνω meaning 'to sweep clean' as Heather was often used to make the bristles of traditional besoms.[104] It can indicate the need for a spiritual clean and tidy up. If this Few appears with Ngeadal / Broom, it highlights an urgent need for a deep clean in your home or in an aspect of your life.

The Heather is famous for its beautiful though small flowers which are in bloom between July and September, so the plant is not actually in flower at the time of the Summer Solstice, the time it rules in *The Celtic Tree Calendar*. Usually, its flowers come in shades of mauve, but they can also be white.

Heather is seen as a very lucky plant, so when Heather is cast, it shows a time of good fortune and many blessings. However, to truly understand its lucky reputation we need to take a look at some old folklore. To find white Heather is considered very lucky, but to pick or wear white Heather will only bring you terrible misfortune.[105] This is because white Heather is said to only grow on the graves of dead fairies, so if you pick it, you will be dishonouring their dead and incurring the full wrath of the fairies. So here Heather warns us to be careful how we make our luck and never to try to steal it from others. Heather is abundant and so shows us there are more than enough blessings around for everyone.

Our ancestors saw the time when the Heather flowers as a season of rejoicing and indulgence, thanks to Heather honey and Heather ale. Heather is telling you now is a good time to celebrate and treat yourself to a little indulgence. Heather ale became the stuff of legend. It is thought that it was in fact not an ale, but a mead, made from Heather honey and it was infamously potent stuff. The resultant inebriation was not just getting drunk in celebration, it was reputed to bring on mystical or psychic experiences. The Celts believed that Heather ale did not just break down inhibitions and enable people to live a little more than usual, they believed that it actually broke down the veil between this world and the next, between our inner and outer worlds or between our conscious and subconscious.

In some ways Heather is the grave, the earth in which we are buried for it is the open threshold between live and death, rather like Ruis, but in reality, it is the threshold between conscious and subconscious mind, between our inner and outer selves. It is the doorway between the spiritual and the physical through which we can bring our dreams into reality. Today witches may use Heather in their magic to enhance their psychic skills or keep a sprig with their tools. Ur in a reading suggests incredible psychic and spiritual development that will truly take you to the next level.

Heather symbolises joy, love, passion, sensual pleasure and the enjoyment of life. A bed of Heather is where love is usually consummated in Celtic myths, such as in the tale of Diarmuid and Graine – one of Ireland's greatest romances. Ur represents long term and meaningful love. It usually tends to represent couples but it can represent other sorts of partnerships too. It may indicate a new love, rekindling your passion, be it for a person or a hobby that you have not had much of a chance to indulge in of late. Heather asks you to show your partner some love, show them just how much they mean to you, how much you appreciate them, how grateful you are that they are in your life and how happy they make you. Romance them, time for a date or movie night or quality time, just the two of you. To keep love alive we need to fuel it, just as you need to fuel a fire. In a relationship Heather says to be yourself, do not try to be anyone else and do not try to change others to suit you.

Alternatively, Heather may be asking you to find or rekindle your passion and zest for love. Perhaps Heather is telling you to seek out new things that will fill you with love and happiness, such as a new job that you will love it you find that you are really not enjoying the one you currently have. Find out what you love doing and give it all your heart.

Heather is associated with the Earth and Mother Goddess Anu, The Welsh Love Goddess Branwen and the Romano-Celtic Goddess Uroica, who seems to have been revered in what is now Switzerland. Uroica derives from a combination of the Celtic and Greco-Roman terms for Heather, *ur* and *ereice*. Uroica was seen as a sort of Queen Bee at Midsummer whose hive was sustained by the nectar of the Heather. Like a bee loyal to their queen and hive, Heather encourages you to be loyal to the one you love, to your friends and colleagues who rely on you.

As Heather is the smallest of the trees and plants of the Ogham; it shows us how to appreciate and find great joy in little things. This allows us to always find something to inspire or uplift us, even when the bigger things may seem to be trying to bring us and our mood down. Getting into the habit of being able to find joy in the little things can bring meaningful healing, especially for your soul.

Due to its very close link with the earth, Heather provides us a way of working with Mother Earth. Heather makes a friendly guide for anyone wishing to deepen their connection to the sacred land on which they live, and to learn the mysteries and magic of the ancient land. Heather teaches us how to ground or earth ourself, and to be more down to earth, for it is one with the earth. If you are having trouble grounding yourself after magical workings or feeling too away with the fairies, Heather can bring you gently, but firmly back to earth.

Ur Reversed

When Heather is reversed it suggests unhappiness and a lack of love. May suggest an issue that you and your partner need to work through; let things progress naturally, and keep talking to each other kindly and from the heart. May indicate a lack of self-love or a blow to your self-esteem or self-confidence. You are feeling dissatisfied with your life and may need to make some changes to find things, such as a new job, that will bring you satisfaction and restore your love for life.

Edhadh – Aspen

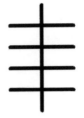

Letter: E
Original Meaning: Unknown
Keywords: Fear, Doubt, Listening to Inner Self, Protection
Tree Type in Brehon Laws: Lower Division
Celtic Tree Calendar: Sep 21ˢᵗ (Autumn Equinox)
Element: Air
Deity: Rhiannon, Pwyll and Arawn
Bird Ogham: Swan
Other Animal: White Mare
Colour Ogham: Red
Other Colour: Grey
People Ogham: Four Children
Crystal: Obsidian
Planet: Saturn

Word Oghams & Other Sources
Cuchulainn: *'Kin of the Birch.'*
Oenghus: *'Synonym for a friend.'*
Morann Mac Main: *'Distinguished wood. A name for the trembling tree.'*
The Song of Amergin: 'I am the shield for every head.'

General Explanation
The original meaning of Edhadh is unknown, which just adds to the mystery of this Few. It has been assigned the Aspen, a tree

synonymous with friendship, trembling, fear, courage and the Underworld. The Aspen is a very unusual tree; it is deciduous, yet tends to like growing with coniferous trees, rather than deciduous trees like itself. In this respect it could be seen as a bit of a loner or a rebel. The Aspen grows in clonal colonies, which were all born from a single seedling and then developed and spread via root suckers. While each individual tree may only live for up to one hundred and fifty years, the root system can live much longer and produce more clones. One such root system in Utah is reputed to be an amazing eighty thousand years old.[106]

The Aspen has quite a dark, sombre and Otherworldly appearance. The trunk appears dark, black sometimes, the bark is a dark grey and the leaves too have a rather grey appearance. In a reading Aspen may portend a time of darkness, depression, disappointments and disheartening circumstances, but it also reminds you that you will survive this and come out the other end wiser and stronger.

Aspens are best known for their 'quaking' or 'trembling' appearance as the foliage shakes in the wind as a result of their flattened petioles, which are designed to reduce aerodynamic drag on the trunk and branches. According to folklore the Aspen trembles as a result of the trauma of having witnessed the Crucifixion of Christ.[107] In another version the Aspen was cursed by God to tremble until Judgement Day for refusing to weep over Christ's death. Due to its lore the Aspen has become deeply associated with fear and death. Aspen asks you what do you fear? If you need to work through fear, anxiety or trauma, Aspen encourages you to seek the help that you need. Take good care of your mental health. Remove yourself where possible from situations and people that are making you fearful. Listen to your inner fears and anxieties, work through them and move on. Aspen shows you how your fears are impacting your life, affecting your judgement and holding you back. You can and will conquer your fears, for there is nothing to fear but fear itself. In the meantime, face your fears with courage and do it anyway.

In modern magic the Aspen, being a tree of the Underworld due to its complex root system, is linked with the Welsh Deities Pwyll and Rhiannon. Pwyll – the Prince of Dyfed, once encountered Arawn – the King of the Underworld while out hunting and ended up running the Underworld for a year. Pwyll did not fear the Underworld or death to which it is so closely linked, for all its morbid reputation, he just got on and did the job he was asked to do to the best of his abilities, which impressed the real King of the Underworld no end. A while later Pwyll heard tell of a fairy mound which if sat upon at a certain time of year would show the person something important. This vision would either terrify the person into complete insanity or instil them with great wonder.[108] Pwyll did not fear the power of the mound; he refused to allow its reputation to scare him and so he decided to try his luck and sat upon the mound. This is why Aspen seeks for us to understand what it is we truly fear, are we scared of something real, or just the smoke and mirrors?

What Pwyll saw whilst upon this mound was Rhiannon, a beautiful Fairy Queen who became his wife and mother to their child. Years later when their son was born, the child was taken away by a monster. Rhiannon's maids panicked, not wanting to be blamed. They smeared poor Rhiannon with blood and placed bones before her so she and others would think Rhiannon had killed him.[109] The maids wanted to create horror and fear, to make Rhiannon scared of herself, and to make the people of Dyfed scared of her. However, like Pwyll, Rhiannon did not give into her fears, she followed that inner voice that told her that she would never do such a thing. It is later revealed that the child is alive and well, and the family are reunited. Here Aspen shows us to listen to our inner voice for guidance, no matter what the rest of the world is trying to fool us into thinking. You know yourself best and what you are capable or not capable of.

For centuries the Aspen was used to make shields, just as *The Song of Amergin* infers, so Aspen offers to protect us from fear and to help bring out our inner courage. As the whispering tree, Aspen urges you to listen to the inner voice that encourages you rather than the one that instils doubts and fears. Do not fear the unknown, seek to understand it. Knowledge, courage and inner strength are all key to conquering our fears. Aspen was used in the past as a painkiller and so can metaphorically and spiritually assist us with dealing with the very real pain caused by our fears and anxieties. Aspen tells us not to suffer, but to get the help and advice we need to overcome and learn from our fears.

In the past, the Autumn Equinox, which is ruled by the Aspen in *The Celtic Tree Calendar*, was a genuinely worrying time for many. The Autumn Equinox is the second Harvest Festival and in times past people were often quite fearful as to whether or not they would have enough resources to see them through the Winter. Aspen urges to plan ahead to make preparations for lean times, rainy days, or our own metaphorical Winter, to make sure that we have the things we will need to confidently get us through.

The Aspen was also the wood used to make the sticks that were used to measure people for coffins and graves and so gained an unlucky or morbid reputation, yet the Aspen was also said to protect people, especially from theft.[110]

With the rustling of its leaves, the Aspen is a master of the wisdom of the air and speaks continually of its mysteries, as well as those of the forest, as long as there is a breath of wind. All we have to do is listen. As Ailm is the Few of expressing ourselves, Edhadh as the Aspen is the Few of listening. Bring quietude to your life so that you can hear the wisdom that is being shared with you. Listen carefully to the advice and messages you are receiving and pay them heed where appropriate. Perhaps try meditation to still your mind and open your ears. Listen to the whisperings of nature. What do they say to you?

In everything it represents Aspen highly recommends that you seek help and advice from those who can help you. Do not suffer in silence. Do not suffer alone. As Aspens form their own support network, seek out like-minded souls and form your own protective support network, if you do not already have one.

Edhadh Reversed

When it presents in reverse, Aspen indicates that your fears are taking you to a really dark place. These fears are very real and disturbing for you, but Aspen questions do they really need to be? Are these fears based in reality or are they born from your own insecurities? Perhaps you are being oversensitive or perhaps you do not understand the situation well enough to be able to see past your fears? It is vital that you do not give in to your fears. By all means use them to be wary, cautious and sensible, but utilise them – do not let them use you.

Idho – Yew

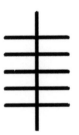

Letter: I / Y
Original Meaning: Yew or Evergreen
Keywords: Transition, Eternal Life, Gateway, Coming Full Circle
Tree Type in Brehon Laws: Chieftain
Celtic Tree Calendar: December 21st to 22nd (Midwinter Solstice)
Element: Earth
Deity: Ankou, Arawn, Ceridwen, Hecate

Bird Ogham: Eaglet
Other Animal: Spider
Colour Ogham: White
Other Colours: Black and very Dark Green
People Ogham: Five Children
Crystal: Malachite
Planet: Saturn

Word Oghams & Other Sources
Cuchulainn: *'Colour of a sick man, agedness.'*
Oenghus: *'Fairest of the ancients.'*
Morann Mac Main: *'Oldest of woods.'*
The Song of Amergin: 'I am the tomb of every hope.'

General Explanation
In *The Ogham Tract* both Edhadh and Idho are listed as Yew in different places, but it is Idho that seems to truly be the Yew, for in the Art Ogham it is listed as *ibroracht* or 'Yew woodworking'.[111]

With Edhadh / Aspen we faced and overcame our fears, so now with Idho / Yew we are ready to face our final fate. To the Celts the Yew symbolised eternal life. The Yew is an evergreen with small spiky dark green leaves, flaky brown bark, and bright red berries which are actually seed cones. All parts of the Yew are extremely toxic and so the Yew is considered a tree of death, as well as eternal life. Yew trees can live for an extraordinary length of time; the Fortingall Yew in Perthshire is said to be a staggering nine thousand years old.[112] Even in its grand old age, and even when dying, the Yew is always a beautiful, inspiring and commanding sight. The Yew is indeed the *'fairest of the ancients'* as Oenghus so elegantly put it.

In Britain the Yew is synonymous with tombs, graves and churchyards for that is where they are most often found, but in many cases, it appears the Yew trees are much older than the churches and chapels they stand near. According to Breton folklore the Yew grows a root into the open mouth of every corpse in the graveyard. This root symbolises the rebirth of the spirits of the dead into the Otherworld.

The Yew lives so long because of its remarkable ability to continually renew itself in a cycle that must have seemed to our ancestors as if it was eternal. Its branches grow down to the ground, take root and form new stems which then arise up around the original trunk as separate but still linked entities. When the core of the original tree rots, a branch will tend to turn inwards and root, living off the decaying and composting nutrients of the original mother tree. This is why the Yew is such an enduring symbol of the cycle of life, death and rebirth, and the new that arises and is nourished by the old.

Furthermore, the Yew represents the life that is in death and the death in the midst of life, for the two are always connected and always circling around and within each other. Due to this association the Yew in *The Celtic Tree Calendar* rules over the darkest night on the year, in which the rebirth of the light is seeded, the Midwinter Solstice. For new things to grow, for new things to happen, other things must give way or even die. Here the Yew challenges you to look at your life, at the beginnings and endings and how the cycle of life is playing out in your life. What do you want to do moving forward? What must you give up in order to start these new things?

The Yew symbolises and connects us to our ancestors and ancestral wisdom. Here Yew refers to your immediate ancestors, those still with you who are in their grand old age, those you have loved and lost, and those ancient ancestors that stretch back through the eons and about whom you may know absolutely nothing. If you are seeking advice, Yew inspires you to go to your elders and your ancestors. Alternatively, the Yew may be asking you to look to your own past, or perhaps your own past lives. Do not repeat your own mistakes and do not repeat the mistakes of others. Learn from them and build a better future.

Our ancestors and elders hold a wealth of information. For centuries such wisdom was passed on by word of mouth rather than through the written word. To be able to store and carry such information garnered serious respect. It was via word of mouth and memory that the Druids kept and shared their knowledge and how the wisdom of the Ogham was preserved until it was first written down, may years after it had first been created. Yew recommends that we look to our memories, to remember those who have made us who we are and to look to the treasure of knowledge that we are building up within ourselves that we may well pass on in the future. Yew asks us an important question: after you pass away, how do you want to be remembered? How will others actually remember you, based on your words and deeds? Will you be remembered as an honourable or good person? What legacy will you leave for your descendants and for the world at large?

The Yew is a tree linked to Ankou – the Breton Spirit or God of Death. He is in many ways the original Death, with his skeletal body, black cloak and scythe. To some he is a cursed spirit, doomed to wandering the world collecting the souls of the dead, to others he is a very kindly soul who calmly guides and accompanies us on our last journey so we will not be lonely or lost. Ankou is very much a protector of the dead and not necessarily to be feared. In Welsh legend the King of the Dead is Arawn, about whom little is known other than he appears to be quite an honourable king. As the Goddess who presides over the death of Gwion and his rebirth as Taliesin, Ceridwen is sometimes linked to this Few, as is the Greek Goddess of the Crossroads, the Dead and Magic – Hecate.

In Celtic legends the Yew often gave shelter to or inspired wisdom in to those who were sick, dying, had lost their sanity or were in desperate need. It was on wands of Yew that the Druid Dalan carved his Ogham to locate Etain, so it may be that Yew was originally used to create Ogham Fews for divination.

According to Welsh folklore the tree the God Llew takes shelter in the form of an eagle after he is wounded by a spear is a Yew and in Irish legend Fionn Mac Cumhaill and his men – the Fianna, meet their end in The Valley of the Yew. As Yews are involved, Fionn and his men are, of course, not actually dead, they are just sleeping. They will arise again with full vigour at Ireland's greatest hour of need and save the day.

The Yew symbolises transition, from one state of being to the next and the passage of time. When Yew is cast it shows that a major transition or change is coming. A phase of your life, a relationship, an old way of thinking, old beliefs or biases, a project or a set of circumstances could be drawing to its natural end. This change may be good, it may not be, but whatever it is it will be significant and will have long term implications for you, your family and any others who are involved. It is an opportune time to shed those things which are no longer of use to you, to clear out the old to make way for the new. This could be traumas, emotions or people who have caused you distress or it could be literal stuff in the form of books that you no longer need that are just cluttering up your living space.

On the other side of the death and endings symbolised by the Yew is new life, rebirth and – as we have reached the end of the original Ogham – the gateway leads us back to Beith and new beginnings. Congratulations, you have come full circle and become older and wiser.

Idho Reversed

Yew reversed suggests that you are too busy dwelling in the past to make the most of the present or even to think of the future. It is fine to reminisce and remember the past, but we cannot live there. You may be actively trying to avoid or delay inevitable changes, but you are wasting your time. All you are doing is holding yourself back. These changes need to happen for things and for you to move forward. Accept them rather than fight them. Seek the positive in what may appear negative at first glance. There may be a major change in the direction of your life. You may feel as if you are being taken in completely the wrong direction, but rest assured it will work out in the end. There is light and life at the end of the tunnel.

Chapter 11

The Forfeda

These are the later additions to the Ogham, and so there is generally less information available on them. Many scholars, diviners and magical practitioners ignore them or even discredit them. There is some confusion over which symbol refers to which tree, or even if it refers to a tree at all. I have included them here to help you to get a full overview of all the Ogham Fews available to you. It is your choice as to whether you use them in your divination or not.

Ebhadh – Elecampane

Letter: EA
Original Meaning: The Salmon of Wisdom, Elecampane
Keywords: A Treat, Indulgence, Sweet Joy, Fairy Magic
Celtic Tree Calendar: The Fairy Festivals
Element: Earth
Deity: Those who are also Fairy Monarchs
Animals: Stag, Ousel
Colour: Yellow
Crystal: Fluorite
Planet: Earth and Sun

Word Oghams
Cuchulainn: *'Fairest fish.'*
Oenghus: *'Corrective of a sick man.'*

General Explanation
The etymology of Ebhadh, also written Eadhadh, is unclear, although it appears to be very similar to Edhadh whose origins are also a mystery. According to Morann Mac Main, this Few refers both to salmon, most likely the Salmon of Wisdom, whose story we looked at under Coll / Hazel, and the Aspen tree with its buoyant wood. Oenghus also describes it as the Aspen. Yet both Morann and Oenghus have already listed the Aspen as Edhadh within the fourth Aicme. Perhaps the two similar sounding names Edhadh and Ebhadh have led to this confusing duplication.

For this book, to avoid duplication, I have followed the lead of the earlier part of *The Ogham Tract* which lists Ebhadh as Elecampane. Throughout the ages Elecampane has borne many enigmatic names such as Elf Dock, Elf Wort, Scabwort, Wild Sunflower, Horseheal and Velvet Dock.[113] Its official name is *Inula helenium*, after Helen of Troy. According to Greek legend, Helen was gathering this herb when she was abducted from Sparta by Paris[114] and the plant is said to have sprung up where her tears fell.

Elecampane is a rather large and stout herbaceous plant that can reach heights of about one to one and a half metres high. Elecampane prefers moist and damp conditions and tends to be found growing somewhat sporadically. It is sadly not a particularly widespread or common herb these days, although it was cultivated far more in the past for its healing properties.

Elecampane is one of the Sunflower family and produces large bright yellow flower heads from June to August. It produces large oval shaped leaves, which can be up to thirty centimetres long and twelve centimetres wide. These leaves are green on the topside and scattered with hairs, while the underside is white and woolly. Its root, which was once highly sought after by confectioners, is thick, succulent has a distinctive sweet and camphor-like scent.

Throughout Mediaeval Europe the roots were candied and eaten as a sweet delicacy. Decoctions of it were also used to sweeten the breath. When Elecampane appears in a reading, it indicates that life is sweet or in need of some sweetening up. Everything seems to be going very well for you right now. Things are going as planned, people seem keen to work with you and help you, there are plenty of opportunities, your health is good and you feel happy with life and with yourself. As things are going so well, you can afford to take a few moments for yourself and really treat yourself. Maybe book a spa day, read a good book, indulge in a little confectionary or take your partner out on a romantic date. It will lift your spirits, feel rejuvenating and provide you with good cheer. *'Elecampane will the spirits sustain'*,[115] according to one Mediaeval saying.

Elecampane speaks of heartfelt happiness, the kind that warms and enlivens us deep within. You are feeling loved and blessed. In modern magic Elecampane is often used in love spells, healing spells and for fairy magic. It has long been rumoured to be a powerful aphrodisiac. Every great herbalist for the last thousand years has written of Elecampane's medicinal properties. It has antibacterial and anti-inflammatory properties, and it has been used to lift the mood, help digestion, for treating asthma and other respiratory complaints, sciatica, skin diseases, liver complaints as well as for countless other maladies.

Elecampane has long been considered a sacred plant of the fairies, hence its bynames of Elf Dock and Elf Wort. It has become closely connected to the Fairy Festivals of Beltane and Midsummer's Eve, when its magical properties are said to be at their most potent. The Saxons used Elecampane to treat Elf-shot,[116] which was a name given to any kind of ache or pain with a sudden onset, things like cramps or sciatica. According to folklore fairies and elves were reputed to live under[117] or take shelter under the plant. This association between Elecampane, fairies and magic seems to be widespread; in Russian the plant is known by the wonderful name of Девясил ('Magic Power'). The Celts too considered Elecampane a magical and sacred plant.[118] If you are seeking advice, Elecampane recommends that you seek your answers from the fairies and the spirits of the land and look to the old fairy stories for inspiration.

As a fairy plant, Elecampane speaks to us of the protection, magic and blessings of the fairies. You are being blessed and protected by the spirits of nature at this time, that is why life seems to be so sweet and magical. It is important when working with the fairies and spirits of nature to acknowledge their help and show gratitude, but do not use the phrase 'thank you' as they take it as an insult. Rather leave biodegradable offerings and do the things that will really help the fairies out, such as cleaning up litter in the woods or taking care of plants that they love. Now is a great time to open up the channel of communication with the fairies and local land spirits, when this Few appears it may mean that they are seeking to work with you or share something with you. Be respectful and willing to learn and they will share their magic with you.

A great time to practice magic or divination. Your psychic skills are at their most powerful and the insights you gain will be profound. A fortuitous time to perform ceremonies or to perform blessings, such as blessing your home or car. You are like the Elecampane, a life form that is rooted to and in the earth, but that reaches up joyfully to the heavens in search of spiritual enlightenment.

Ebhadh Reversed

When reversed, Elecampane suggests bitterness, misfortune or misunderstanding. Clear the air and resolve any misunderstandings. You may be feeling bitter about things, or someone else may be directing their bitterness at you. Now is a time for forgiveness; let that bitterness go for its wasting too much of your energy and time. Instead believe in yourself, believe that things can and will get better and believe in the blessings and magic of nature and the spirits of nature that are all around you. Reach out to the spirits of the land and open your heart to them and to the blessings and wisdom that they offer. If you feel that your misfortune may be the result of accidentally angering the local land spirits, reach out to them, apologise and leave a suitable offering.

Oir – Spindle

Letter: OI
Original Meaning: Gold
Keywords: Hearth, Home, Family, Honour
Tree Type in Brehon Laws: Lower Division
Element: Earth / Fire
Deity: Dagda
Colour: Gold
Animal: Deer, Golden Plover
Crystal: Gold
Planet: Moon

Word Oghams
Oenghus: *'Beauty of form, heath.'*

Morann Mac Main: *'Most venerable of structures/substances.'*

General Explanation

The Common Spindle or *Euonymus europaeus* is a small, shrubby deciduous tree that is most often found today in public parks because it is considered a beautiful and ornamental tree. Traditionally though it has tended to grow in hedgerows or on the edges of the woods, and is a big fan of chalky soils. If you are lucky enough to spot a Spindle tree in a hedgerow or woodland, it may indicate that the hedgerow or woodland is a very ancient one. Its leaves are a waxy, shiny, serrated and green, though they turn vibrant shades of orange and red before falling come the Autumn. The Spindle produces small, hermaphrodite, yellow-green flowers in May and June which are then pollinated by insects before developing into bright pink and very poisonous pop-corn-like fruits with orange seeds.

While the Spindle appears pretty and delicate, the wood of the Spindle tree is very hard. As charcoal it is famed for both its density and strength. There is a folk belief that anything touched with the wood of the Spindle will not go bad, which is why it was used to make skewers for food.[119] As well as skewers, in the past the wood was used to make pegs, toothpicks, bobbins and was synonymous with the crafting of spindles for spinning, which is where the British English name of the tree comes from. As spinning was seen as a very domestic endeavour and often carried out by the hearth fire, over time the Spindle has become a tree linked to hearth, home and family. The Spindle tree, the family and the home can all be considered *'the most venerable of structures'* after all. Perhaps it is due to its link with abundance and the family that has led to it being so closely linked to the great Father of the Gods in Irish Legend – the Dagda.

In a reading, Spindle calls on you to tend carefully and lovingly to your hearth and home, to the physical building and to your family. Make any repairs that you need to, either in terms of

DIY or repairing your relationship with your nearest and dearest. Spindle asks you are you spending enough time at home or with your family? Do you have a good work/life balance or is your homelife suffering for the sake of your work life? Do you feel at home within your residence or is it just a house to you? Do what you need to do to make your house feel like a home.

Although the word *Oir* means 'Gold', Spindle warns us against giving in to the pressures of the modern materialistic world. Material goods are all very well and good when they suit a purpose and are needed, but they can be cumbersome, expensive and take up valuable space in our lives. Spindle encourages us to use what we have rather than always looking to get more stuff. To reuse items and give them new life and to repair what is broken rather than always looking to rush out to replace everything with the latest model. Here Spindle speaks of our impact on the planet and its resources, and the terrible wasteland of refuse we are turning the planet into. Spindle reminds us of the things that really matter, like family, happiness and good health, which are far more valuable than possessions or gold could ever be. Here, Spindle calls on you to re-evaluate your relationship with your stuff and your family. Re-evaluate your relationship with money and your perceptions of wealth. Make room in your life and in your heart for the things that really matter, such as the things, the experiences and the people that really make you feel blessed and happy.

If you are seeking advice, Spindle requests that you ask your family for their input and advice. When it comes to families, we have two: we have the family we are born into and then the family that we choose for ourselves. As adults we get to choose who we allow into our homes and hearts. Spindle advises us to forge deep and long-lasting connections with those we choose to make our family. This applies as much to our extended family of friends as it does to our partner and children. Fulfil your obligations to those that you hold dear in your heart. Keep the promises you have made, attend the events you said you would and do the chores you already agreed to. Be honourable, compassionate and kind in your dealings with your loved ones. Let them know you truly care for them. Help them out when you can and support them wholeheartedly when they are pursuing goals or dreams, even if you think it is all just a fantasy or a water of their time.

The botanical name of the Spindle, *Euonymus*, is Greek and means 'Good Name', as in a person's honour. Spindle can indicate a need to honour existing obligations and commitments before taking on any new ones. Honour is often represented by the Spindle; here it urges you to look at your personal honour and that of your family. Are you acting honourably towards others and are others acting honourably towards you? This is an ideal time to work on your honour, to help others in a kind and honourable way.

Spindle shows a great time for engaging with your family or to create one if you do not already have one. May also indicate the forging of new friendships, some great new opportunities to get more involved with your local community or suggest engaging with new groups with whom you share a common interest such as an art group, a spiritual community, or a support group for any illness you may have. It will give you a fantastic chance to learn from others and help others in a productive, supportive cycle that benefits everyone. If you are already involved with such groups, the Spindle encourages you to keep engaging with them, for any group is only as strong as the sense of community forged by its members.

The Spindle does really stand out in the woods or hedgerows when its unusual fruits appear and so represents individuality and non-conformity. Do not feel like you have to be like everyone else, to have the latest things, to be watching the latest popular TV show, or to be married with two kids, if that is not what you want. You are not like everyone else – no one is – it is all a misconception designed to separate us from our hard-earned cash. We are all such unique souls with so much to offer, and that uniqueness is something to be celebrated and embraced, not hidden away.

Spindle Reversed

In this position Spindle indicates that your work/home life has become completely imbalanced. You are spending far too much at work or chasing wealth and not spending enough time at home or with your family. Your attempts to keep up with the rat race are taking a serious toll on your well-being and your relationships. This is an urgent wake-up call to engage with your family, to honour the promises you have made to them and to spend time with them while you can, because no one knows what the future may hold. You or others are acting with dishonour and Karma will soon be knocking at the door unless this is quickly remedied.

Uillean – Honeysuckle

Letter: UI
Original Meaning: Elbow
Keywords: Live Life to the Full, Love, Fidelity, The Search for the Self
Celtic Tree Calendar: Summertime
Element: Air
Deity: Dagda, Danu
Colour: Pale Yellow

Animal: Lapwing, Mouse
Crystal: Fluorite
Planet: Sun / Moon

Word Oghams

Oenghus: *'Great equal-length, woodbine, i.e., honeysuckle.'*
Morann Mac Main: *'Fragrant wood is woodbine, for it is a name for honeysuckle.'*

General Explanation

The name of this Few translates as 'great elbow', and is a reference to the shape of this Few. It is the only Few in the entire Ogham to have a curve, which must have made it very awkward for stone carvers to inscribe.

The Honeysuckle, Woodbine or *Lonicera periclymenum* is a deciduous, flowering plant that can grow to around seven metres tall or more. The Honeysuckle can be found in hedgerows, woodlands and scrubland, but today is often found in gardens as well for its highly valued for its strongly scented flowers and its ability to cover up boring looking walls or fences.

The leaves are oval, green and arranged in pairs. Sometimes in a warmer Winter the leaves will stay on the bush for the duration. In Spring it produces trumpet-like flowers which start out as white, before turning yellow, with a red or pink tinge. The flowers produce a sweet, cloying, warm and fruity fragrance. They produce more scent during the night than they do in the day, so are a favourite of many nocturnal moths and night owls. After the flowers have been pollinated the Honeysuckle forms clusters of bright red berries in Autumn which are very popular with many songbirds.

As its flower is at its best at night, the Honeysuckle has long been linked to the Moon, but it is also a plant of the Sun, for while the Honeysuckle does best where its roots can be in shade, as it grows the plant will reach for the Sun. It is a prolific grower, that twines clockwise as it climbs, either around itself, other plants or whatever structure it is growing up. It can often take over and can distort, damage or kill other plants.

You may feel that your life has been as winding path, full of dead ends, distractions, wasted time and lost opportunities, but Honeysuckle assures you that you are on the right path and making good progress on your journey. Do not compare yourself to others for only you can walk your path in life and everyone's path is different.

Honeysuckle's spiralling search for the Sun has long been likened to the human quest for spirituality, to the search for self and the search for the hidden. Yet the Honeysuckle also warns us to be cautious and sensible in our search, because somethings once seen cannot be unseen. Here Honeysuckle challenges us to know what it is that we are searching for, or at least to have some inkling and to have the courage to keep searching, no matter how long or how far the search takes us.

This is the Few of the quest, just like those undertaken in the old Celtic legends by the Knight of the Round Table, by Fionn Mac Cumhaill and others. What is it that you are questing for or seeking? Are you looking to find your life purpose, your soulmate or your true self? Are you looking to achieve certain goals, to obtain a successful career in a specialist field, to get a degree or write a book? Quests are hard work and may last for many months or even years. They challenge our inner strength, mental resolution, courage, our faith and every part of us, but quests will always reward us with wisdom and experience, even if we do not find the original thing that we were searching for. Honeysuckle allows us to see what is real and what is fake and so will help you to keep true to the quest rather than getting waylaid or entwined with distractions.

The Honeysuckle speaks to us of pursuing our hidden and deep desires. Honeysuckle asks you what is your heart's desire? That one thing that you really, really want in life and would give everything for. How will you go about achieving it? How will you turn your hope or dream into reality? When Honeysuckle appears, it may indicate that you are or need to be following your heart's desire. This is a good time to allow yourself to pursue your desires and your dreams.

One of the great things about the Honeysuckle is that sometimes it shows us that the great hidden secrets that we have spent ages, if not a lifetime, or even perhaps lifetimes, searching for can in fact be right there in plain sight and under our nose, and not hidden at all. This is very true of our search for the self. Honeysuckle encourages us to search for our real, authentic self – who we really are on the inside. Not that person you pretended or pretend to be at school work or out in public, but the real you. When you cast Honeysuckle, it is always urging you to be true to yourself and your feelings.

The Honeysuckle is perceived as a lucky and protective plant. It was believed that if Honeysuckle grew around a window or door that its presence would stop evil fairies, witches and spirits from entering the home. This is why Honeysuckle was often hung or grown over doors to homes and barns for protection.

As the plant twines and entwines the Honeysuckle is a Few of love, of the passionate embrace and the way we hold others dear to our hearts. It believed that Honeysuckle represents the love that entwines two people together, especially when that love is romantic and passionate.[120] In Shakespeare's *A Midsummer Night's Dream,* Titania speaks of encircling Bottom in her arms: '*So doth the woodbine the sweet honeysuckle gently entwist*'.[121] Honeysuckle's link with love is considered so powerful that in Victorian times young ladies were banned from bringing any Honeysuckle into the house for fear that it would inspire dreams of passion. Young men would seek out walking sticks or 'twisties' that featured Honeysuckle, for such sticks were reputed to bring luck in love.[122]

In *The Language of Flowers,* the Honeysuckle symbolises deep fidelity and devoted love.[123] When Honeysuckle appears in your reading, it can represent a time of great passion, of great love and finding or deepening your connection with your soul mate. Spend this time with your partner as much as you can, sharing and caring and enjoying your love together. Love unites us, it binds and entwines us together, just as the Honeysuckle does.

Uillean Reversed

You may be feeling as if your entire life is coming apart. There may be separations. You are experiencing loss and becoming distracted from your life plan. Honeysuckle offers you a chance to get your life back on track by following your heart and staying true to your values. You may be feeling lonely or unloved, or worse still, unworthy of love. Honeysuckle assures you that you are loved and worthy of great love. The façade that you wear for others is oppressing you and strangling the life out of the real you. Discover your inner self once again; nurture and love it so that you may find joy.

Iphin – Gooseberry

Letter: PH, then later IO
Original Meaning: Spiny
Keywords: Children, Inner Child, Nurturing
Element: Air / Earth
Colour: Green
Animal: Caterpillar

Deity: The Gooseberry Wife, Brighid, Arianrhod
Planet: Venus

Word Oghams

Oenghus: *'Most wonderful of taste, gooseberry.'*
Morann Mac Main: *'Sweetest tree.'*

General Explanation

The word *Iphin* derives from an old Irish term for 'Spiny', which perfectly fits the Gooseberry. The Gooseberry is a straggly shrub that usually grows no more than about one and a half metres high and has distinctive spines which can do some nasty damage to human skin. They can be found in hedgerows, on the edges of woodland and riverbanks. Gooseberries can also be found being cultivated for their fruit in people's gardens and were a far more popular food in the past than they seem to be today.

The leaves are lobed, a little like those of the Hawthorn, while the flowers are a greenish-cream, often with hints of pink. The hairy fruit appears very early in the year, often starting out in April and being ripe by mid-June. Their fruits can be yellow, green, red or even purple depending in its cultivar. The berry has long been used to make cordials, wine, jams, pies and puddings such as the gooseberry fool. When raw the gooseberry tastes like tart grapes, but it becomes much sweeter once cooked.

Traditionally the Gooseberry has been used as a remedy for various ailments. The berry is rich in vitamin C and other nutrients and has anti-inflammatory properties, so has been used to treat wounds, arthritis, coughs, colds, digestive complaints and many more maladies. Perhaps because of the strange little hairs on the berries, the Gooseberry is still used today is some shampoo formulations designed to help invigorate the scalp and reduce hair loss.

The folklore surrounding the Gooseberry often implies

protection and healing. In Britain there is the somewhat bizarre saying *'May the skin of a Gooseberry cover all your enemies'.* In Ireland one cure for warts was to prick them with a Gooseberry thorn and to throw it away. A Gooseberry thorn would be pointed at a stye on the eyelid and the word 'away' would be chanted three times to banish it.[124]

Throughout Britain there is tell of a fairy who is connected to the Gooseberry bush. In Yorkshire she is known as Awd Goggin and on the Isle of Wight she is called The Gooseberry Wife. She is said to take the form of a large and woolly caterpillar who munches on the leaves of the Gooseberry all the while protecting the plant from marauding children who want to eat its berries.[125] She was even said to eat children who ate too many of the precious berries!

The Gooseberry has a close link with children, who often love the energy of this plant, hence I guess why it needs some protection from them from the Gooseberry Wife. When British children ask their parents where babies come from, one flippant answer often given by adults who do not wish to explain the details and rob their child of innocence is *'under a Gooseberry bush'.* Of course, the Gooseberry bush here is a euphemism to where children really do come from.[126] Whatever its origins, the link between children and Gooseberry bushes is a close one. In the past children loved Gooseberrying, which can refer to either picking the fruit, most of which goes straight in their mouths, or the prank whereby you steal a person's washing from the line. There was once a children's rhyme that featured the Gooseberry. In its original form it went like this:

'Here we go round the Gooseberry bush,
The Gooseberry bush,
The Gooseberry bush,
Here we go round the Gooseberry bush,
On a cold and frosty morning.'

Over time the Gooseberry was replaced with the Mulberry[127] and became the version still sung by children today.

Gooseberry in a reading may infer matters of women's cycles, birth or children. Gooseberry is a plant associated with the Celtic Goddess of Healing and Midwifery – Brighid and with Arianrhod – the Welsh Goddess of Rebirth, both of whom were often called upon by Midwives and women in labour. The children that the Gooseberry Few refers to may mean your own children, your nieces and nephews, other children that you interact with, such as any children that you teach or babysit, or your own inner child. It can also refer to a child who is on the way or whom you plan to have in the future.

The message here is to spend more time with your children or more time tending your own inner child. Do the things with your children that really matter: make memories with them, talk to them, read to them and show them how much you love them. They will only be children once and while every parent wants to be there to watch their children grow up, it is your choice as to whether you do so or not. If you are struggling to find time to be with your children, Gooseberry is telling you very firmly to make time, quit making excuses and do it, or else this time and their childhoods will have passed you by before you know it.

As we grow up, many of us lose our connection with our inner child, or find our inner child has become hurt or traumatised by life. Gooseberry calls on us to spend time and energy to heal and nurture our inner child and to reconnect to them through the activities we enjoyed doing as a child. Sing your favourite song from childhood, play your favourite game or read your favourite book. Engage with an old childhood friend. If you have children ask them what their favourite things are and engage with them through those things. It will also be fun to share your own favourites with your children.

As the Gooseberry bears a sweet fruit so beloved by children, it reminds us to be sweet and kind to our inner child and to the other children we encounter in life. Protect their happiness and innocence when you can, but also allow them to make the most of this precious stage of life and develop the understanding they will need to be a successful adult when the time comes. Gooseberry embodies the sweetness of the ideal childhood, and helps us to be kind and sweet to our inner child – especially if our own childhood was not sweetness and light for any reason. Allow your inner child to bloom, even if it was not allowed to do so back then.

If you are seeking answers or advice, the Gooseberry suggests you ask the children in your life or your inner child. Children understand the world deeply in their own way. They make excellent teachers for they take us back to what really matters in life. They may offer you a great insight or enable you to see things from an entirely different perspective.

Iphin Reversed

When reversed the Gooseberry intimates that you have lost touch with your inner child, or are losing touch with the children in your life. May also indicate the need to protect your children or inner child. You may feel very distanced from your children, after all, childhood today is nothing like the childhood we had only a few decades ago because the world has changed so drastically. Let your child teach you about their modern childhood and let you know what they need from you as their loving parent. Despite the additional age and experience, be open to the fact that parents do not always know best. Talk to your child or inner child and listen to what they have to say.

Eamhancholl – Twin of Coll

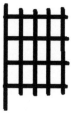

Letter: CH (as in the Scottish 'Loch'), X and later AE
Original Meaning: Twin of Coll or Witch-Hazel / Wych Elm
Keywords: Magic, Death, Healing, Omens
Deity: Dana / Donn
Element: Water / Earth
Colour: Mouse-coloured, Grey
Animal: Salmon of Wisdom
Crystal: Tourmaline
Planet: Moon

Word Oghams

Oenghus: *'Corrective of a sick man.'*
Morann Mac Main: *'Expression of a weary one, ach, ah! uch, alas!'*
Battle of the Trees: *'The elm with his retinue, Did not go aside a foot, He would fight with the centre, And the flanks, and the rear.'*

General Explanation

The word *Eamhancholl* means 'Twin of the Hazel' and is depicted as what looks like two Coll Fews placed together. The Twin of Hazel that *The Ogham Tract* refers to is the British Witch-Hazel also known as the Wych Elm or *Ulmus glabra,* which is not the same as the American Witch-Hazel at all.

The Wych Elm is a deciduous tree that has a broad crown and buds and twigs that are covered in orange hairs. Its leaves have serrated edges, an asymmetrical base and taper to a fine point.

Their topside is rough to the touch. The Wych Elm produces clusters of hermaphrodite flowers which appear before the leaves in Spring and are red-purple in colour. Once pollinated the flowers develop into small winged fruits called samaras which contain a single seed at their centre. These winged seeds soon dry out, turn brown and are carried away by the wind. Most Wych Elms do not even start to produce their fruit until they reach forty years of age and so are an inspiration for late bloomers in life and those who believe that 'Life begins at forty!'

Once upon a time the majestic Elm reached the height of around thirty or even forty metres and was one of the most common trees in Ireland and Britain. Sadly, many of Britain and Ireland's Wych Elms were decimated by Dutch Elm disease which arrived in 1919 CE and has not been eradicated. As a result, many of the Wych Elms that exist today are younger and still somewhat smaller than the mature specimens that were lost. This concept of the Wych Elm being linked to death is nothing new, as the Wych Elm has been viewed as a tree of death for centuries. For generations Wych Elm was the favoured wood for coffins, as it not only has a very beautiful grain, it is also very long-lasting, even in the damp ground, and so was thought to help protect the deceased.

Like Straif /Blackthorn and Ruis / Elder, the Elm refers to death, endings and completion. As with the other Fews, this is not meant to be macabre, rather it is that death is a gateway to another realm or to rebirth. It is the end that leads to a new beginning. Wych Elm offers us a deep understanding of this that is not morbid or depressing but full of wisdom, acceptance and even appreciation.

In Celtic mythology the Wych Elm was a tree of the Underworld and the Fairy Otherworld as it was reputed to grow near and guard various portals into these other realms such as in graveyards, on barrows or on fairy mounds.[128] So closely were the fairies linked to the Wych Elm by the Celts, the Saxons and the Norse that one old byname for the tree was simply 'Elven'.[129]

Some viewed the Wych Elm as downright murderous. With its pliancy, the Wych Elm was the favoured wood for the making of longbows by the Welsh and longbows were a lethal and effective weapon in Mediaeval warfare. In Taliesin's *Battle of the Trees*, he hails the Wych Elm as a great fighter. Furthermore, the Elm tree itself has the reputation of killing or trying to kill people as it has the reputation for very suddenly dropping large boughs on fine and still days which led to the somewhat ominous phrase '*Elm hateth man, and waiteth...*'[130] The Wych Elm reminds us of our own mortality, how things can change in an instant, and the cycle of life, death and rebirth. Yet Wych Elm is also a tree of life and healing. According to Norse legend the first woman, Embla, was created from a fallen Elm tree[131] and during the Mediaeval era the Wych Elm was considered a panacea – able to heal all ailments known to human or beast.

Back when Elms grew to majestic proportions, many were often given specific names, as we still find today with Oak trees, and were used as landmarks or way markers. In the East Riding of Yorkshire there were the musical Elms known as Tenor, Bass and Alto which marked the route to the village of Sigglesthorne.[132] As a way marker Wych Elm can help guide you in life. It can indicate that you are undergoing a change or transition in life or taking a whole new direction. Wych Elm may appear at a time when you are feeling lost or waylaid in order to help call your attention to this and assist you with getting back on track. If you are currently planning anything, such as a journey, new project, career or house move, Wych Elm suggests you make a plan with set way markers to help and guide you. When Wych Elm appears, it can portend journeys and travel of all kinds.

The Wych Elm is a tree of omens and divination, which are another kind of way marker, and calls for you to pay extra attention to the omens and messages you are receiving at the moment. If a Wych Elm were to drop its leaves ahead of Autumn, it was an omen of plague or other disease. Forked branches of Wych Elm have long been used for water-witching, the art of divining for water.[133] The Saxons so linked the Elm to omens and divination that King Edgar, when he was calling for the ban of tree worship stated that *'Divination with the dead, omens and charms with songs...are practised on elms and various other trees.'*[134] The Wych Elm has always been a tree of magic and witchcraft, even though the Wych part actually derives from the Old English *wice*, meaning 'pliant' or 'supple', which is cognate with *wicker*, rather than the magical practitioner. According to folklore witches were said to both shun the Elm[135] and use its branches for their wands.[136]

The Wych Elm is sacred to the Mother of the Gods known to the Welsh as Don and to the Irish as Dana – the mother of the *Tuatha Dé Danann* ('the Tribe of Dana').[137] She is a truly ancient Mother Goddess and Goddess of the Earth and perhaps also of Water, for some believe that Danu is the same as the Vedic Goddess Danu who lent her name to several European rivers such as the Don, Danube and Dnieper. Water is the element most associated with the Wych Elm because, like the Alder, it withstands water and dampness very well. In the past it was used to make dowsing rods, cartwheels, the hulls of boats, and the foundation pilings for bridges. At one point hollowed out Elm was used to make utility pipes, which provided clean water to countless homes.

The Wych Elm has always been one of those trees that the hedge witch, gardener or farmer looks to for advice and friendship, for it is so closely linked with the earth, with water and with the cycle of life, death and rebirth that plays out in the gardens, fields and hedgerows each year. There is a wealth of agricultural lore associated with the Wych Elm, such as *'When the elmen leaf is as big as an ear, then sow barley never fear.'*[138]

Eamhancholl Reversed

You may be feeling distracted, lost, confused or out of touch. Seek those things which feel or seem like familiar markers to help you get on your way again. This could be the Stars above, the routine of your day job, you partner as your anchor in life, a familiar hobby or anything that gives you a sense of place and safety, from where you can then begin to journey once more. You are attempting to resist change or you misunderstand the changes that are occurring. Work with Wych Elm to embrace and understand these changes and what they mean to you.

Part IV

Pronunciation Guide

Aicme – 'Ahk-me'
Aicmi – 'Ahk-mi'
Ailm – 'Ahlem'
Beith – 'Beh'
Coll – 'Kull'
Duir – 'Doo-r'
Eamhancholl – 'Eh-van-CHoll' with the CH as in the Scottish 'Loch'
Ebhadh – 'Ev-yah'
Edhadh – 'Eh-yah'
Fearn – 'Fairn'
Feda – 'Fay-dah'
Flesc – 'Flayshk'
Gort – 'Gurt'
Iphin – 'E-fin'
Luis – 'Loo-urs'
Muinn – 'Mwin'
Ngeadal – 'Nyayh-tl'
Nin – 'Nin'
Nuinn – 'Nyuhn'
Ogham – 'Oh-am'
Oir – 'Oir' or 'Aur'
Onn – 'Ohn'
Quert – 'Ki-errt'
Ruis – 'Ris' or 'Roo-ish'
Saille – 'Sahl-yuh'
Straif – 'Strayf'
Tinne – 'Chin-yuh'
Uillean – 'Ill-ahn'
Ur – 'Uhr'
Ydho – 'Ee-yoh'

References

1. Jones, M. (2003) *Jones's Celtic Encyclopedia*. Oghma Grainainech

2. Ryan, C. (2012) *Border States in the Work of Tom Mac Intyre: A Paleo-Postmodern Perspective*. United Kingdom: Cambridge Scholars. pp. 204-5

3. McManus, D. *Ogam: Archaizing, Orthography and the Authenticity of the Manuscript Key to the Alphabet*, Ériu 37, 1988, 1–31. Ireland: Royal Irish Academy

4. O'Kelly, M.J. (1989) *Early Ireland, An Introduction to Prehistory*. United Kingdom: Cambridge University Press. p.251

5. Calder, G. (1917) *Auraicept na n-éces: The Scholars' Primer*. United Kingdom: J. Grant. p.275

6. Graves, R. (1948) *The White Goddess*. United Kingdom: Faber & Faber Ltd. p.216

7. Bane, T. (2014) *Encyclopedia of Imaginary and Mythical Places*. United States: McFarland, Incorporated, Publishers. p.42

8. Frazer, J.G. (2003) *The Golden Bough: A Study of Magic and Religion*. Project Gutenberg. Volume II. p. 358

9. Philpot, J.H. (1897) *The Sacred Tree or The Tree in Religion and Myth*. United Kingdom: MacMillan. pp.93-94

10. Richardson, R.D. & Higgins, R. (2017) *Thoreau and the Language of Trees*. United States: University of California Press. p.54

11. Byghan, Y. (2020) *Sacred and Mythological Animals: A Worldwide Taxonomy*. United States: McFarland, Incorporated, Publishers. p.153

12. Spence, L. (1995) *Druids: Their Origins and History*. United States: Barnes & Noble. pp.58 &160

13. Guest, C. (1877) *The Mabinogion*. United Kingdom: B. Quaritch. p. 471

14. Calder, G. (1917) *Auraicept na n-éces: The Scholars' Primer*. United Kingdom: J. Grant. p. 335
15. Frazer, J.G. (2003) *The Golden Bough: A Study of Magic and Religion*. Project Gutenberg. Chapter X
16. Carmichael, A. (1941) *Carmina Gadelica: Hymns & Incantations*. United Kingdom: T. & A. Constable. p.168
17. Watts, D.C. (2007) Elsevier's Dictionary of Plant Lore. United Kingdom: Elsevier. p.32
18. Znamenski, A.A. (2007) *The Beauty of the Primitive: Shamanism & Western Imagination*. United Kingdom: Oxford University Press. p.135
19. Judd, W.S. (2017) *Flora of Middle-Earth: Plants of J.R.R. Tolkien's Legendarium*. United Kingdom Oxford University Press. p.265
20. McOwan, R. (1990) *Tartans: The Facts & Myths*. United Kingdom: Jarrold. p.7
21. Corrigan, I. (2012) *The Book of Visions*. United Kingdom: Lulu.com. p.76
22. Knight, S. (2008) *Runes*. United States: Sterling Publishing Company. p.380
23. Calder, G. (1917) *Auraicept na n-éces: the Scholars' Primer*. United Kingdom: J. Grant. p.296
24. Bisol, J.L. (2015) *The Golden Alders*. Lulu.com. p.5
25. Munro, R. (2020) *Ancient Scottish Lake-Dwellings or Crannogs*. Germany: Outlook Verlag. p.133
26. Bisol, J.L. (2015) *The Golden Alders*. Lulu.com. p.6
27. Reno, F.D. (2000) *Historic figures of the Arthurian Era: Authenticating the Enemies and Allies of Britain's post-Roman King*. United Kingdom: McFarland & Company. p.96
28. Kerr, A.R.J. (2009) *Ancient Egypt and Us: The Impact of Ancient Egypt on the Modern World*. United States: Ferniehirst Publishing. p.100
29. The British Magazine, Or, Monthly Repository for Gentlemen & Ladies. (n.d.). United Kingdom: James

Rivington & James Fletcher ... & H. Payne. p.483

30. Dietz, S. (2020) *The Complete Language of Flowers: A Definitive and Illustrated History*. United States: Book Sales. p.195

31. Bonica, J.J. (2010). *Bonica's Management of Pain*. Argentina: Lippincott, Williams & Wilkins. p.1157

32. Douce, F. (1807) *Illustrations of Shakespeare, and of Ancient Manners: with Dissertations on the Clowns and Fools of Shakespeare; on the Collection of Popular Tales Entitled Gesta Romanorum; and on the English Morris Dance*. Vol. 1. p.169

33. Dietz, S. (2020) *The Complete Language of Flowers: A Definitive and Illustrated History*. United States: Book Sales. p.195

34. Calder, G. (1917) *Auraicept na n-éces: the Scholars' Primer*. United Kingdom: J. Grant. p.296

35. Hollander, L.M. (2010) *The Poetic Edda*. United States: University of Texas Press. Lay of Grimnir, 36

36. Roderic, D.J. (1862) *Barddas; Or, a Collection of Original Documents, Illustrative of the Theology, Wisdom, and Usages of the Bardo-Druidic System of the Isle of Britain*. United Kingdom: Longman & Co.

37. Lecouteux, C. (2016) *Encyclopedia of Norse and Germanic Folklore, Mythology, and Magic*. United States: Inner Traditions/Bear. Askr

38. Franklin, A. (2016). *Romantic Guide to Handfasting: Rituals, Recipes & Lore*. United States: Llewellyn Worldwide, Limited. Ash

39. Calder, G. (1917) *Auraicept na n-éces: the Scholars' Primer*. United Kingdom: J. Grant. p.291

40. Jennings, S. (2005). *Goddesses*. United Kingdom: Hay House. Olwen

41. Grimassi, R. (2000) *Encyclopedia of Wicca & Witchcraft*. United Kingdom: Llewellyn Publications. p.207

42. Dietz, S. (2020) *The Complete Language of Flowers: A Definitive and Illustrated History*. United States: Book Sales. p.68

43. Lester Packer., L. Wachtel-Galor, S., Choon, N.O. &

Barry Halliwell, B. (2004) *Herbal and Traditional Medicine: Biomolecular and Clinical Aspects*. United States: Taylor & Francis. p.421

44. Simon, K. & King, S. (2018) *Cheshire: Local, Characterful Guides to Britain's Special Places*. United Kingdom: Bradt Travel Guides. p.248

45. Leslie, F. (1866). *The Early Races of Scotland and Their Monuments*. United Kingdom: Edmonston and Douglas. p.68

46. Folkard, R. (1884) *Plant lore, legends and lyrics*. United Kingdom: Sampson, Low. p.467

47. Calder, G. (1917) *Auraicept na n-éces: the Scholars' Primer*. United Kingdom: J. Grant.p.296

48. IBID. p.291

49. Lawrence, E.A. (1997). *Hunting the Wren: Transformation of Bird to Symbol: A Study in Human-Animal Relationships*. United States: University of Tennessee Press. p.23

50. Folkard, R. (1884) *Plant lore, legends and lyrics*. United Kingdom: Sampson, Low. p.467

51. Frazer, J.G. (2003) *The Golden Bough: A Study of Magic and Religion*. Project Gutenberg. Volume II. p.358

52. Bergin, O. (1927) "How the Dagda Got his Magic Staff". *Medieval Studies in Memory of Gertrude Schoepperle Loomis*. Paris & New York. pp. 399–406

53. Guest, C. (1877) The Mabinogion. United Kingdom: B. Quaritch. p.426

54. Mills, D. (2011) *A Dictionary of British Place-Names*. United Kingdom: OUP Oxford.

55. Weatherstone, L. (2015) *Tending Brigid's Flame: Awaken to the Celtic Goddess of Hearth, Temple, and Forge*. United States: Llewellyn Worldwide, Limited. Oak

56. Morgan, K.E. (2016) *Carmarthen Through Time*. United Kingdom: Amberley Publishing.

57. Barefoot, A., Badham, S. & Biddle, M. (2000). *King Arthur's*

Round Table: An Archaeological Investigation. United Kingdom: Boydell Press. p.253

58. Kilic, S. (2021). *Winter Evocations.* Paragon Publishing. p.12
59. Kerrigan, M. (2016) *Celtic Legends: Heroes and Warriors, Myths and Monsters.* United Kingdom: Amber Books Ltd. Fight or Flight
60. Ó hÓgáin, D. *Myth, Legend & Romance: An encyclopaedia of the Irish folk tradition.* Prentice Hall Press, 1991. pp.273-276
61. Lynch, P. (2010) *Tales of Irish Enchantment.* Ireland: Mercier Press. p.80
62. Grimm, W. & Grimm, J. (1999). *Fairy Tales from Grimm.* United Kingdom: Oxford University Press. p.206
63. Trevelyan, M. (1909) *Folk-lore and Folk-stories of Wales.* United Kingdom: E. Stock. p.104
64. Journal of Geomancy. (1977). United Kingdom: Institute of Geomantic Research. p.8
65. Yeats, W.B. (2021). *The Wind Among the Reeds.* United States: West Margin Press. The Song of Wandering Aengus
66. *Duanaire Finn* Poem XVI "The Shield of Fionn", ed. MacNeill (1908), ed. pp. 34–38, tr. pp. 134–139
67. Calder, G. (1917) *Auraicept na n-éces: the Scholars' Primer.* United Kingdom: J. Grant. p.296
68. Bruce, C.W. (1999). *The Arthurian Name Dictionary.* United Kingdom: Garland. p.50
69. Guest, C. (1877) The Mabinogion. United Kingdom: B. Quaritch. p.473
70. Bane, T. (2014) *Encyclopedia of Imaginary and Mythical Places.* United States: McFarland, Incorporated, Publishers. p.57
71. Knight, S. (2000) *Celtic Traditions: Druids, Faeries, and Wiccan Rituals.* United States: Citadel Press/Kensington Publishing Corporation. p.91
72. Unknown (before 1250) *Llyfr Du Caerfyrddin / The Black Book of Carmarthen.* National Library of Wales. *Yr Afallennau / The Apple Trees*

73. Guiley, R. (2006) *The Encyclopedia of Magic and Alchemy*. United States: Facts On File, Incorporated. p.16

74. Dietz, S. (2020) *The Complete Language of Flowers: A Definitive and Illustrated History*. United States: Book Sales. p.191

75. McGarry, M. (2021) *Irish Customs and Rituals: How Our Ancestors Celebrated Life and the Seasons*. Ireland: Orpen Press. Michaelmas

76. Weatherstone, L. (2015) *Tending Brigid's Flame: Awaken to the Celtic Goddess of Hearth, Temple, and Forge*. United States: Llewellyn Worldwide, Limited. Plants

77. Wolverton, B.C., Douglas, W.L. & Bounds, K. (September 1989). *Interior landscape plants for indoor air pollution abatement* (Report). NASA. NASA-TM-101766

78. Dietz, S. (2020). *The Complete Language of Flowers: A Definitive and Illustrated History*. United States: Book Sales. p.103

79. Calder, G. (1917) *Auraicept na n-éces: the Scholars' Primer*. United Kingdom: J. Grant. p.291

80. Dietz, S. (2020) *The Complete Language of Flowers: A Definitive and Illustrated History*. United States: Book Sales. p.103

81. Wagner, R. & Bassett, P. (2006) *Richard Wagner's Tristan and Isolde*. Australia: Wakefield Press. p.7

82. Duke, J. A. (2000) *The Green Pharmacy Herbal Handbook: Your Comprehensive Reference to the Best Herbs for Healing*. United Kingdom: Rodale Books. p.52

83. Guest, C. (1877) The Mabinogion. United Kingdom: B. Quaritch. p.426

84. Dainotto, R.M. (2015) *The Mafia: A Cultural History*. United Kingdom: Reaktion Books. p.106

85. Daniels, C.L. (2003) *Encyclopædia of Superstitions, Folklore, and the Occult Sciences of the World: Volume II*. United States: University Press of the Pacific. p. 639

86. IBID. P.1448

87. Watts, D.C. (2007) Elsevier's Dictionary of Plant Lore.

United Kingdom: Elsevier. p.47

88. Eliade, M. (1978) *The Forge and the Crucible*. United States: University of Chicago Press. p.49

89. White, N.I. (2013) *The Frank C. Brown Collection of NC Folklore: Vol. VII: Popular Beliefs and Superstitions from North Carolina, Pt. 2*. Germany: Duke University Press. p.126

90. Locke, T. (2017) *Tales of the Irish Hedgerows*. United States: History Press

91. IBID

92. McGarry, G. (2000) *Brighid's Healing: Ireland's Celtic Medicine Traditions*. United Kingdom: Green Magic. p.215

93. Lundskow, G. (2008) *The Sociology of Religion: A Substantive and Transdisciplinary Approach*. India: Sage Publications. p.308

94. Gomme, G.L. & Burne, C.S. (1914) *The Handbook of Folklore*. United Kingdom: Folklore Society. p.34

95. *"Pinus longaeva"*. Gymnosperm Database. March 15, 2007

96. Hatfield, G. (2004) *Encyclopedia of Folk Medicine: Old World and New World Traditions*. United Kingdom: ABC-CLIO. p.265

97. Napier, J. (2008) *Western Scottish Folklore & Superstitions*. Lethe Press. p.175

98. Monaghan, P. (1990) The Book of Goddesses & Heroines. United States: Llewellyn Publications. p.380

99. Hatfield, G. (2004). *Encyclopedia of Folk Medicine: Old World and New World Traditions*. United Kingdom: ABC-CLIO. p.70

100. Simpson, J. (2008). A Dictionary of Proverbs. United Kingdom: OUP Oxford

101. *DK Eyewitness Travel Guide: Brittany*. (2011). United Kingdom: Dorling Kindersley Limited. p.29

102. Frazer, J.G. (2003) *The Golden Bough: A Study of Magic and Religion*. Project Gutenberg. Volume I. p.112

103. Calder, G. (1917) *Auraicept na n-éces: the Scholars' Primer*.

United Kingdom: J. Grant. p.296

104. Dietz, S. (2020) *The Complete Language of Flowers: A Definitive and Illustrated History.* United States: Book Sales. p.46

105. *Little Giant Book of Superstitions.* (2008). United States: Sterling Publishing Company. p.265

106. Obrist, H.U., Zimmer, C. & Sussman, R. (2014). *The Oldest Living Things in the World.* United States: University of Chicago Press. p.52

107. Daniels, C.L. (2003). *Encyclopædia of Superstitions, Folklore, and the Occult Sciences of the World*: Volume II. United States: University Press of the Pacific. p.767

108. Guest, C. (1877) The Mabinogion. United Kingdom: B. Quaritch. p.344

109. IBID. p.353

110. Daniels, C.L. (2003). *Encyclopædia of Superstitions, Folklore, and the Occult Sciences of the World*: Volume II. United States: University Press of the Pacific. p.767

112. Trouet, V. (2020). *Tree Story: The History of the World Written in Rings.* United States: Johns Hopkins University Press. p.34

113. Dietz, S. (2020). *The Complete Language of Flowers: A Definitive and Illustrated History.* United States: Book Sales. p.114

114. Castleman, M. (2010). *The New Healing Herbs: The Essential Guide to More Than 125 of Nature's Most Potent Herbal Remedies.* United States: Rodale. p.199

115. Grieve, M., Grieve, M. & Marshall, M. (1971) *A Modern Herbal, Vol. I.* United States: Dover Publications. p.279

116. Wood, M. (2008) *The Earthwise Herbal: A Complete Guide to Old World Medicinal Plants.* United States: North Atlantic Books. p.304

117. Law, D. (1973) *Concise Herbal Encyclopaedia.* United Kingdom: Bartholomew. p.304

118. Richardson, R. (2017) *Britain's Wild Flowers: A Treasury of*

Traditions, Superstitions, Remedies and Literature. United Kingdom: National Trust

119. Daniels, C.L. (2003) *Encyclopædia of Superstitions, Folklore, and the Occult Sciences of the World: Volume II.* United States: University Press of the Pacific. p.844

120. Simpson, J. & Roud, S. (2000) *A Dictionary of English Folklore.* United Kingdom: Oxford University Press. Honeysuckle

121. Shakespeare, W. (2008) *A Midsummer Night's Dream.* United Kingdom: Macmillan Education UK. Act IV: Scene 1

122. Simpson, J. & Roud, S. (2000) *A Dictionary of English Folklore.* United Kingdom: Oxford University Press. Honeysuckle

123. Cumo, C. (2013) *Encyclopedia of Cultivated Plants: From Acacia to Zinnia*: From Acacia to Zinnia. United States: ABC-CLIO. p.498

124. Wilde, F.S. (2018) *Ancient Legends, Mystic Charms, and Superstitions of Ireland.* United States: Create Space. p.152

125. Bane, T. (2013) *Encyclopedia of Fairies in World Folklore and Mythology.* United States: McFarland, Incorporated, Publishers. p.164

126. Cryer, M. (2016) *Superstitions: And Why We Have Them.* New Zealand: Exisle Publishing Limited. p.61

127. Simpson, J. & Roud, S. (2000) *A Dictionary of English Folklore.* United Kingdom: Oxford University Press. Mulberry

128. Sherman, J. (2015) *Storytelling: An Encyclopedia of Mythology and Folklore.* United Kingdom: Taylor & Francis. p.136

129. Dietz, S. (2020). *The Complete Language of Flowers: A Definitive and Illustrated History.* United States: Book Sales. p.223

130. Sherman, J. (2015) *Storytelling: An Encyclopedia of Mythology and Folklore.* United Kingdom: Taylor & Francis. p.136

131. Lecouteux, C. (2016) *Encyclopedia of Norse and Germanic Folklore, Mythology, and Magic.* United States: Inner Traditions/Bear. Embla. Traditions/Bear. Embla

132. Stafford, F.J. & Stafford, F. (2016) *The Long, Long Life of*

Trees. United States: Yale University Press. p.197

133. *Transactions of the Woolhope Naturalists' Field Club*. (1869). United Kingdom: (n.p.). p.83

134. The Gentleman's Magazine Library: *Popular superstitions*. (1968). United States: Singing Tree Press. p.185

135. Sherman, J. (2015) *Storytelling: An Encyclopedia of Mythology and Folklore*. United Kingdom: Taylor & Francis. p.136

136. *Transactions of the Woolhope Naturalists' Field Club*. (1869). United Kingdom: (n.p.). p.83

137. MacLir, A.G. (2012) *Wandlore: The Art of Crafting the Ultimate Magical Tool*. United States: Llewellyn Worldwide, Limited

138. *Transactions of the Woolhope Naturalists' Field Club*. (1869). United Kingdom: (n.p.). p.85

Bibliography

Andersen, H. C. & Haugaard, E. (1977) 'The Elder-Tree Mother or Mother Elderberry', *The Complete Fairy Tales and Stories of Hans Andersen*, London: Victor Gollancz

Bane, T. (2014) *Encyclopedia of Imaginary and Mythical Places.* United States: McFarland, Incorporated, Publishers

Barefoot, A., Badham, S. & Biddle, M. (2000). *King Arthur's Round Table: An Archaeological Investigation.* United Kingdom: Boydell Press

Bergin, O. (1927) "How the Dagda Got his Magic Staff". *Medieval Studies in Memory of Gertrude Schoepperle Loomis.* Paris & New York

Bisol, J.L. (2015) *The Golden Alders.* Lulu.com

Bonica, J.J. (2010). *Bonica's Management of Pain.* Argentina: Lippincott, Williams & Wilkins

The British Magazine, Or, Monthly Repository for Gentlemen & Ladies. (n.d.). United Kingdom: James Rivington & James Fletcher ... & H. Payne

Bruce, C.W. (1999). *The Arthurian Name Dictionary.* United Kingdom: Garland

Byghan, Y. (2020) *Sacred and Mythological Animals: A Worldwide Taxonomy.* United States: McFarland, Incorporated, Publishers

Calder, G. (1917) *Auraicept na n-éces: The Scholars' Primer.* United Kingdom: J. Grant

Carmichael, A. (1941) *Carmina Gadelica: Hymns & Incantations.* United Kingdom: T. & A. Constable

Castleman, M. (2010). *The New Healing Herbs: The Essential Guide to More Than 125 of Nature's Most Potent Herbal Remedies.* United States: Rodale

Corrigan, I. (2012) *The Book of Visions.* United Kingdom: Lulu. com

Cryer, M. (2016) *Superstitions: And Why We Have Them*. New Zealand: Exisle Publishing Limited

Cumo, C. (2013) *Encyclopedia of Cultivated Plants: From Acacia to Zinnia*: From Acacia to Zinnia. United States: ABC-CLIO

Dainotto, R.M. (2015) *The Mafia: A Cultural History*. United Kingdom: Reaktion Books

Daniels, C.L. (2003) *Encyclopædia of Superstitions, Folklore, and the Occult Sciences of the World: Volume II*. United States: University Press of the Pacific

Dietz, S. (2020) *The Complete Language of Flowers: A Definitive and Illustrated History*. United States: Book Sales

DK Eyewitness Travel Guide: Brittany. (2011). United Kingdom: Dorling Kindersley Limited

Douce, F. (1807) *Illustrations of Shakespeare, and of Ancient Manners: with Dissertations on the Clowns and Fools of Shakespeare; on the Collection of Popular Tales Entitled Gesta Romanorum; and on the English Morris Dance*. Vol. 1

Duke, J. A. (2000) *The Green Pharmacy Herbal Handbook: Your Comprehensive Reference to the Best Herbs for Healing*. United Kingdom: Rodale Books

Duanaire Finn Poem XVI "The Shield of Fionn", ed. MacNeill (1908), ed.

Eliade, M. (1978) *The Forge and the Crucible*. United States: University of Chicago Press

Folkard, R. (1884) *Plant lore, legends and lyrics*. United Kingdom: Sampson, Low

Franklin, A. (2016). *Romantic Guide to Handfasting: Rituals, Recipes & Lore*. United States: Llewellyn Worldwide, Limited

Frazer, J.G. (2003) *The Golden Bough: A Study of Magic and Religion*. Project Gutenberg

Gomme, G.L. & Burne, C.S. (1914) *The Handbook of Folklore*. United Kingdom: Folklore Society

Graves, R. (1948) *The White Goddess*. United Kingdom: Faber & Faber Ltd

Grieve, M., Grieve, M. & Marshall, M. (1971) *A Modern Herbal, Vol. I.* United States: Dover Publications

Grimassi, R. (2000) *Encyclopedia of Wicca & Witchcraft.* United Kingdom: Llewellyn Publications

Grimm, W. & Grimm, J. (1999). *Fairy Tales from Grimm.* United Kingdom: Oxford University Press

Guest, C. (1877) The Mabinogion. United Kingdom: B. Quaritch

Guiley, R. (2006) *The Encyclopedia of Magic and Alchemy.* United States: Facts On File, Incorporated

Hatfield, G. (2004) *Encyclopedia of Folk Medicine: Old World and New World Traditions.* United Kingdom: ABC-CLIO

Hollander, L. M. (2010) *The Poetic Edda.* United States: University of Texas Press.

Jennings, S. (2005). Goddesses. United Kingdom: Hay House

Jones, M. (2003) *Jones's Celtic Encyclopedia.*

Journal of Geomancy. (1977). United Kingdom: Institute of Geomantic Research

Judd, W.S. (2017) *Flora of Middle-Earth: Plants of J.R.R. Tolkien's Legendarium.* United Kingdom Oxford University Press

Kerr, A.R.J. (2009) *Ancient Egypt and Us: The Impact of Ancient Egypt on the Modern World.* United States: Ferniehirst Publishing

Kerrigan, M. (2016) *Celtic Legends: Heroes and Warriors, Myths and Monsters.* United Kingdom: Amber Books Ltd.

Kilic, S. (2021). *Winter Evocations.* Paragon Publishing

Knight, S. (2000) *Celtic Traditions: Druids, Faeries, and Wiccan Rituals.* United States: Citadel Press/Kensington Publishing Corporation

Knight, S. (2008) *Runes.* United States: Sterling Publishing Company

Law, D. (1973) *Concise Herbal Encyclopaedia.* United Kingdom: Bartholomew

Lawrence, E.A. (1997). *Hunting the Wren: Transformation of Bird to Symbol: A Study in Human-Animal Relationships.* United

States: University of Tennessee Press

Lecouteux, C. (2016) *Encyclopedia of Norse and Germanic Folklore, Mythology, and Magic*. United States: Inner Traditions/Bear

Leslie, F. (1866). *The Early Races of Scotland and Their Monuments*. United Kingdom: Edmonston and Douglas

Lester Packer., L. Wachtel-Galor, S., Choon, N.O. & Barry Halliwell, B. (2004) *Herbal and Traditional Medicine: Biomolecular and Clinical Aspects*. United States: Taylor & Francis

Little Giant Book of Superstitions. (2008). United States: Sterling Publishing Company

Locke, T. (2017) *Tales of the Irish Hedgerows*. United States: History Press

Lundskow, G. (2008) *The Sociology of Religion: A Substantive and Transdisciplinary Approach*. India: Sage Publications

Lynch, P. (2010) *Tales of Irish Enchantment*. Ireland: Mercier Press

McGarry, G. (2000) *Brighid's Healing: Ireland's Celtic Medicine Traditions*. United Kingdom: Green Magic

McGarry, M. (2021) *Irish Customs and Rituals: How Our Ancestors Celebrated Life and the Seasons*. Ireland: Orpen Press

McManus, D. *Ogam: Archaizing, Orthography and the Authenticity of the Manuscript Key to the Alphabet*, Ériu 37, 1988, 1–31. Ireland: Royal Irish Academy

McOwan, R. (1990) *Tartans: The Facts & Myths*. United Kingdom: Jarrold

Mills, D. (2011) *A Dictionary of British Place-Names*. United Kingdom: OUP Oxford

Monaghan, P. (1990) The Book of Goddesses & Heroines. United States: Llewellyn Publications

Ó hÓgáin, D. *Myth, Legend & Romance: An encyclopaedia of the Irish folk tradition*. Prentice Hall Press, 1991

O'Kelly, M.J. (1989) *Early Ireland, An Introduction to Prehistory*. United Kingdom: Cambridge University Press

Obrist, H.U., Zimmer, C. & Sussman, R. (2014). *The Oldest Living Things in the World*. United States: University of Chicago Press

Morgan, K.E. (2016) *Carmarthen Through Time*. United Kingdom: Amberley Publishing.

Munro, R. (2020) *Ancient Scottish Lake-Dwellings or Crannogs*. Germany: Outlook Verlag.

Napier, J. (2008) *Western Scottish Folklore & Superstitions*. Lethe Press

Philpot, J.H. (1897) *The Sacred Tree or The Tree in Religion and Myth*. United Kingdom: MacMillan

Reno, F.D. (2000) *Historic figures of the Arthurian Era: Authenticating the Enemies and Allies of Britain's post-Roman King*. United Kingdom: McFarland & Company

Richardson, R. (2017) *Britain's Wild Flowers: A Treasury of Traditions, Superstitions, Remedies and Literature*. United Kingdom: National Trust

Richardson, R.D. & Higgins, R. (2017) *Thoreau and the Language of Trees*. United States: University of California Press

Roderic, D.J. (1862) *Barddas; Or, a Collection of Original Documents, Illustrative of the Theology, Wisdom, and Usages of the Bardo-Druidic System of the Isle of Britain*. United Kingdom: Longman & Co.

Ryan, C. (2012) *Border States in the Work of Tom Mac Intyre: A Paleo-Postmodern Perspective*. United Kingdom: Cambridge Scholars

Shakespeare, W. (2008) *A Midsummer Night's Dream*. United Kingdom: Macmillan Education UK. Sherman, J. (2015) *Storytelling: An Encyclopedia of Mythology and Folklore*. United Kingdom: Taylor & Francis

Simon, K. & King, S. (2018) *Cheshire: Local, Characterful Guides to Britain's Special Places*. United Kingdom: Bradt Travel Guides

Simpson, J. (2008). A Dictionary of Proverbs. United Kingdom: OUP Oxford

Simpson, J. & Roud, S. (2000) *A Dictionary of English Folklore*. United Kingdom: Oxford University Press. Honeysuckle

Stafford, F.J. & Stafford, F. (2016) *The Long, Long Life of Trees*. United States: Yale University Press

Spence, L. (1995) *Druids: Their Origins and History*. United States: Barnes & Noble

Transactions of the Woolhope Naturalists' Field Club. (1869). United Kingdom: (n.p.)

Trevelyan, M. (1909) *Folk-lore and Folk-stories of Wales*. United Kingdom: E. Stock

Trouet, V. (2020). *Tree Story: The History of the World Written in Rings*. United States: Johns Hopkins University Press

Unknown (before 1250) *Llyfr Du Caerfyrdd* in / *The Black Book of Carmarthen*. National Library of Wales. *Yr Afallennau / The Apple Trees*

Wagner, R. & Bassett, P. (2006) *Richard Wagner's Tristan and Isolde*. Australia: Wakefield Press

Watts, D.C. (2007) Elsevier's Dictionary of Plant Lore. United Kingdom: Elsevier

Weatherstone, L. (2015) *Tending Brigid's Flame: Awaken to the Celtic Goddess of Hearth, Temple, and Forge*. United States: Llewellyn Worldwide, Limited

White, N.I. (2013) *The Frank C. Brown Collection of NC Folklore: Vol. VII: Popular Beliefs and Superstitions from North Carolina, Pt. 2*. Germany: Duke University Press

Wilde, F.S. (2018) *Ancient Legends, Mystic Charms, and Superstitions of Ireland*. United States: Create Space

Wolverton, B.C., Douglas, W.L. & Bounds, K. (September 1989). *Interior landscape plants for indoor air pollution abatement* (Report). NASA. NASA-TM-101766

Wood, M. (2008) *The Earthwise Herbal: A Complete Guide to Old World Medicinal Plants*. United States: North Atlantic Books

Yeats, W.B. (2021). *The Wind Among the Reeds*. United States: West Margin Press. The Song of Wandering Aengus

Znamenski, A.A. (2007) *The Beauty of the Primitive: Shamanism & Western Imagination*. United Kingdom: Oxford University Press

Websites

Online Copies of Various Sources

https://archive.org/details/auraicept00calduoft/
An online copy of Calder's translation of *Auraicept na n-Éces* (*'The Scholar's Primer'*), including *Lebor Ogaim* (*'The Ogham Tract'*) which records many of the different Oghams.

http://www.ancienttexts.org/library/celtic/ctexts/t08.html
Online copy of *Cad Goddeu* (*'The Battle of the Trees'*)

http://www.equinox-project.com/ogamscales.htm
The Ogham Scales from *Leabhar Bhaile an Mhóta* (*'The Book of Ballymote'*).

http://titus.uni-frankfurt.de/ogam/index.html
Images of the stones carved with Ogham

https://www.babelstone.co.uk/Blog/2013/06/ogham-stones-of-scotland.html
Images, transcriptions and translations of the Ogham stones of Scotland. Those from Wales, England and the Isle of Man are also available on this blog.

General Ogham Resources

http://www.evertype.com/standards/og/ogmharc.html
Calls itself every Ogham thing on the web and there is a lot of great information to explore listed here. Should keep you busy...

http://www.evertype.com/celtscript/ogfont.html
Ogham Fonts

https://www.trustedtarot.com/spirit-guides/ogham/
Free online Ogham Divination, ideal for on the go.

Information on Trees

https://www.treecouncil.ie/native-irish-trees Lots of info on Native Irish Trees, including those of the Ogham.

http://www.the-tree.org.uk Lots of info on British Trees, including those of the Ogham.

https://www.ranker.com/list/songs-about-trees/ranker-music List of songs about or featuring trees. It is not exhaustive, but is a good place to start.

Ogham Quick Reference Sheet

Name	Tree	Keywords	Reversed	Calendar	Deity
Beith	Birch	beginnings, initiation	stuck in a rut	Dec 24 - Jan 20	Arianrhod
Luis	Rowan	protection, inspiration	open to attack	Jan 21 - Feb 17	Rhiannon/Brighid/Taranis
Fearn	Alder	guidance, shield	poor advice	Mar 18 - Apr 14	Bran
Saille	Willow	intuition, emotions	carried away	Apr 15 - May 12	Cerridwen
Nuinn	Ash	order, harmony	no control, separation	Feb 18 - Mar 17	Manannan/Gwydion
Huathe	Hawthorn	obstruction, obstacles	barriers, bad luck	May 13 - Jun 9	Olwen
Duir	Oak	protection, strength	lack of honour	Jun 10 - Jul 17	Dagda/Taranis
Tinne	Holly	patience, testing	vulnerabilities	Jul 18 - Aug 4	Llew/Lugh
Coll	Hazel	wisdom, inspiration	misunderstandings	Aug 5 - Sep 1	Oengus/Brighid
Quert	Apple	health, healing, love	ill-health, exhaustion	Sep 2 - Sep 29	Ceridwen/Morgan/Oenghus
Muinn	Bramble	healing, abundance	greed, lack of luck	Sep 2 - Sep 29	Brighid
Gort	Ivy	restriction, binding	selfishness	Sep 30 – Oct 27	Arianrhod
Ngeadal	Broom	healing, cleansing	illness, unease	Oct 28 - Nov 24	Blodeuwedd/Brighid/Airmid
Straif	Blackthorn	strife, negativity, conflict	endings, death	Nov 1 Samhain	Cailleach/Morrighan
Ruis	Elder	Karma, transition	soul searching	Nov 25 - Dec 21	Arianrhod/Elder Mother
Ailm	Pine	expression, perception	feeling hurt or ignored	Dec 23 Yule	Druantia/Ogma
Onn	Gorse	vitality, optimism	disillusionment	Mar 21 & Aug 1	Llew/Lugh
Ur	Heather	passion, partnership	unhappiness	Jun 21 Solstice	Grainne/Anu/Uroica
Edhadh	Aspen	fear, doubt, protection	darker emotions	Sep 21 Equinox	Rhiannon/Pwyll/Arawn
Idho	Yew	transition, gateway	living in past	Dec 21-22 Solstice	Ankou/Arawn/Ceridwen
Ebhadh	Elecampane	indulgence, joy	misfortune, bitterness		Fairy Monarchs
Oir	Spindle	hearth, home, family	dishonour, distance		Dagda
Uilleari	Honeysuckle	living life to the full, love	distractions, loss	summertime	Dagda/Danu
Iphin	Gooseberry	children, inner child	losing touch		GooseberryWife/Brighid
Eamhancoll	Wych Elm	magic, omens	overwhelmed		Danu/Don

219

MOON
BOOKS

PAGANISM & SHAMANISM

What is Paganism? A religion, a spirituality, an alternative belief system, nature worship? You can find support for all these definitions (and many more) in dictionaries, encyclopaedias, and text books of religion, but subscribe to any one and the truth will evade you. Above all Paganism is a creative pursuit, an encounter with reality, an exploration of meaning and an expression of the soul. Druids, Heathens, Wiccans and others, all contribute their insights and literary riches to the Pagan tradition. Moon Books invites you to begin or to deepen your own encounter, right here, right now.

If you have enjoyed this book, why not tell other readers by posting a review on your preferred book site.

Medicine for the Soul
The Complete Book of Shamanic Healing
Ross Heaven
All you will ever need to know about shamanic healing and how to
become your own shaman...
Paperback: 978-1-78099-419-2 ebook: 978-1-78099-420-8

Shaman Pathways – The Druid Shaman
Exploring the Celtic Otherworld
Danu Forest
A practical guide to Celtic shamanism with exercises and
techniques as well as traditional lore for exploring the Celtic
Otherworld.
Paperback: 978-1-78099-615-8 ebook: 978-1-78099-616-5

Traditional Witchcraft for the Woods and Forests
A Witch's Guide to the Woodland with Guided Meditations and
Pathworking
Mélusine Draco
A Witch's guide to walking alone in the woods, with guided
meditations and pathworking.
Paperback: 978-1-84694-803-9 ebook: 978-1-84694-804-6

Wild Earth, Wild Soul
A Manual for an Ecstatic Culture
Bill Pfeiffer
Imagine a nature-based culture so alive and so connected,
spreading like wildfire. This book is the first flame...
Paperback: 978-1-78099-187-0 ebook: 978-1-78099-188-7

Naming the Goddess
Trevor Greenfield
Naming the Goddess is written by over eighty adherents and
scholars of Goddess and Goddess Spirituality.
Paperback: 978-1-78279-476-9 ebook: 978-1-78279-475-2

Shapeshifting into Higher Consciousness
Heal and Transform Yourself and Our World with Ancient
Shamanic and Modern Methods
Llyn Roberts
Ancient and modern methods that you can use every day to
transform yourself and make a positive difference in the world.
Paperback: 978-1-84694-843-5 ebook: 978-1-84694-844-2

Readers of ebooks can buy or view any of these bestsellers by
clicking on the live link in the title. Most titles are published in
paperback and as an ebook. Paperbacks are available in traditional
bookshops. Both print and ebook formats are available online.

Find more titles and sign up to our readers' newsletter at
http://www.johnhuntpublishing.com/paganism
Follow us on Facebook at https://www.facebook.com/MoonBooks
and Twitter at https://twitter.com/MoonBooksJHP